Being Adam Golightly

One man's bumpy voyage to
the other side of grief

Published in 2018 by
Short Books, Unit 316, ScreenWorks, 22 Highbury Grove,
London, N5 2ER

10 9 8 7 6 5 4 3 2 1

A CIP catalogue record for this book
is available from the British Library.

ISBN: 978-1-78072-316-7

Cover design by Two Associates Ltd
Printed at CPI Group (UK) Ltd, Croydon, CR0 4YY

For Helen – you know how much.

"Somewhere on the other side of this wide night and the distance between us, I am thinking of you."

Carol Ann Duffy

Contents

PROLOGUE

If Adam Golightly had never been born things would be brilliant. It would mean a totally different upbringing for my children Millie (aged 14) and Matt (aged 10) because their mother Helen, my soul mate of 26 years, wife for 17 of them, would not have died of fucking cancer in her 40s.

By "different" I mean remarkably ordinary and yet splendidly happy, with Helen very much alive at the centre of our little world.

However, Helen did die and her death begat Adam Golightly, my pseudonym for my weekly "Widower of the Parish" column in *The Guardian*.

I'd never written like this before. Conceived in the darkness of my grief, Adam became pallbearer, confidant, cheerleader, psychoanalyst, pimp and pathfinder for the rebuild of our little family.

Creating Adam was in many ways a desperate act as I looked for anything which might help me deal with overwhelming grief, leaving me strong enough to support the kids. It seems selfish but I had little consideration of any consequences, good or bad, for the stakeholders in the sharing of our story. It was just a way to anchor me in the present when all I really wanted was to hide like an animal and lick the wounds of my loss.

The column tracked my journey from the day of Helen's death through the pathos, comedy and occasional slapstick of my just-about-coping without her. I featured the children's changing lives, the high and lows of domestic chaos, professional meltdown then reconstruction and the surprise of my emotional hunger and raging libido.

Once I'd started writing, the words flew out of me with an ease and honesty which, though personally painful, I'd begun to hope would somehow help nameless others who tripped over Adam's journey in the paper or online.

I had little feedback at first, until a Twitter account was attached. Suddenly some of the scale and diversity of people's immersion in my story became movingly apparent and I am so grateful for their trust and support.

Then the final column published Adam's e-mail address and I became the recipient of thousands of other people's support and stories of their own loss. I heard from poor souls with life-limiting illnesses, usually fucking cancer, and from scared, articulate and lovely people whose partners have deadly illnesses and see in Adam some hope of a life beyond the worst happening. Further outside the shadows of illness have been regular *Guardian* readers who've laughed, cried and occasionally sniggered at Adam's antics, or people with other adversities, not health related, but who still see in him a cheerleader for a positive future when everything seems hopeless.

Finally and very surprisingly there were those who had not experienced any adversity but lived with a nagging doubt that their lives should be happier. By reading "Widower of the Parish", they found in Adam Golightly a life coach – although death coach might be closer, given my new-found experience of the membrane-thin fragility of life.

This book is so much more than the sum of the columns and I hope you will be able to take out of it whatever you need – bereavement guidebook, checklist for the mid-life crisis you never allowed yourself but always wanted, life-coaching notes or just maybe a chance to shout *hero, villain, arsehole, brave-heart* at the page while hoping it's the sort of thing that doesn't happen to you.

More than anything *Being Adam Golightly* is about living, not dying. It's a celebration of the life we are creating in Helen's long shadow. I love the world as never before and in this book I throw my arms around it and squeeze, until it squeaks.

If I seem, through Adam, to cope sometimes just a bit too well or laugh too much I'll point you to the words of the awesome Albert Schweitzer:

> *The willow which bends to the tempest, often escapes better than the oak which resists it; and so in great calamities, it sometimes happens that light and frivolous spirits recover their elasticity and presence of mind sooner than those of a loftier character.*

"Adam" x

1.

LOVE & LASAGNA

"**I**t's another lady for you, Dad!"

So chimes my young son Matt, having easily reached the front door before me. On our step stands a woman of about 40, well dressed, with coal-black, shoulder-length hair, flashing dark eyes and a nervous air. Beautiful already, she was outstanding for two very different reasons – I'd never seen her before in my life and she was brandishing what looked like a very large dish full to brimming with lasagna.

There's an awkward pause as I look into her eyes, hoping for any spark of recognition to deliver up dialogue and lift the weighty silence between us. Nothing. We continue staring at one other and I notice a slight tremor in her arms, bending under the burden of cast-iron cookware.

I'm better with cars than names or faces, so flick a glance at her shiny blue, newish Mercedes slewn across my drive but don't recognise it either. However, the momentary unshackling of our locked eyes liberates speech...

Dark Stranger: *For you.*

Simultaneously, she thrusts the dish hard at me. As I take it, her now-free arms encircle my shoulders in a long, surprisingly strong hug before she kisses me hard on the cheek and steps deftly back.

The silence recommences and we stare once again into each other's red-rimmed eyes. The tableau has not altered, other than that the dish has changed hands and, as I discover later, there's a ruby-red lipstick-embossed pucker on my unshaven cheek.

Ten days earlier, this encounter might have had a whiff of small-town scandal, but not now.

Bad things don't just happen to other people – they happened to our little family. Helen, my beautiful wife and brilliant mother to Millie and Matt, had died a week earlier. From nowhere, the slight pain in her side had turned out to be not gallstones but a rare bastard form of fucking cancer that would prove deadly in less than two treatment-packed years.

So I was at home with the kids in the eye of the storm; sitting between the worst day ever of having to tell them their mum had died and her funeral – the busyness around which didn't begin to disguise the fact that a sink hole had opened in our wonderfully ordinary lives.

This terrible time was punctuated by a constant stream of cards, calls and callers on our doorstep as news of our loss skewered the complacency of the comfortable community in which we had lived for more than 10 fabulous years.

People are well intentioned; I try to be welcoming, answering them all with varying degrees of monosyllabic turns-of-phrase and unkempt appearance – pyjamas that might be mistaken for leisurewear helping to soften the impact of my dishevelment.

Callers include some of our oldest friends, more recent but close friends and almost-acquaintances. Hats off to them all for overcoming British reserve and "reaching out" as our less inhibited American cousins might say.

Still, having plucked up the kindness and courage to come round, people are often struck dumb on the doorstep. I'm churlish in my grief and feel a little put out by the constant and uncomfortable intrusions and share this fact with my friend Laura. Older than me and a people watcher with an HR background, she sheds some light and shoots from her hip.

Me: *Have I become some sort of freak show? People turn up, shut up and stare or hand something over and scarper.*

Laura: *Come on, you. These are massive statements of friends' shock, support and love for Helen and you all – don't expect people to be articulate and don't judge the encounter by normal social rules – silence, tears, flight and grub are all expressions of great concern.*

Me: *OK, OK! I get it but what do I say to them? How do I get them to bugger off if they don't talk?*

Laura: *Your wife has just died, you don't have to perform, be chatty or even civil. Don't overthink it. They're not coming round to make life harder but just want to help and you may need that help some day soon. Try and get over yourself and be glad – they are beautiful not bad!*

I'm self-aware enough to know my frustrations are as abnormal as everything around me since Helen died. My sober, ostensibly "coping" Dr Jekyll self can't really accept that I'm planning Helen's funeral, a fact that only my drunken Mr Hyde alter-ego can deal with. So morning callers have been facing a hybrid, heavily hungover version of me that hasn't made for chattiness. Now though, chastened by Laura's wise words, I'm making more effort on the doorstep and do so again, although not knowing this caller's connection or even her name doesn't help.

Me (whispering): *Thank you so much for thinking of us.*
Dark Stranger (sniff).
Me: *It really is very kind and looks lovely*
Dark Stranger (sniffs again, tears beginning to flow).

So I step forward and with some sleight of hand manage to hug her with the dish held behind and tight to her back. After long moments of calm and comfort I step back with shaking arms from the weight of the lasagna which I hope hasn't marked her jacket. She's smiling now and quite red in the face and I wonder if she's spotted that I'm actually wearing PJs. Then she leans in and kisses my other cheek before turning smartly on her pointy heels and with just a whiff of Gucci and gravy, heads back towards her Mercedes.

I stare after her departing back, wondering if there's lipstick on my face. Waving as I close the door on the moving car, I turn to Matt who has been watching with his usual forensic attention from the kitchen:

Me: *Any idea who that was?*

Matt: *No idea, Dad, but there's a marble cake in the fridge from someone who knew Mum. She rang the bell when you were in the toilet. Do you know there's lipstick on your face?*

Me: *Who was it?*

Matt: *Nice woman, yellow hair, white car. Looked upset. What's for breakfast?*

Worryingly he's already displaying the nonchalance towards grieving callers of one who has grown up too much in the past few days.

So the lasagna woman remains a mystery. I still have her posh dish. I didn't even look for or notice a wedding ring to provide any small clue if she is the wife of a colleague or work connection of Helen's, perhaps, who can't make it to the funeral next week. Maybe they'll phone. Anyway the die is cast and as the week rolls on there comes a carb rush of calories and a cavalcade of kisses as I find myself comforting and being comforted by a series of well-wishers bearing food and love.

I'm reminded of Matt Damon in the film *We Bought a Zoo*. He's a recent widower who's dismissive of such doorstep gifts; lasagna piles up in his fridge. Soon afterwards he makes some big decisions to move his life on by binning his job and buying his zoo, stroked along the way by the good luck of having Scarlett Johansson as his head keeper.

It's the first, but far from last time I spot how sometimes life can parallel the creativity of fiction but can be even more surprising (being fair, the film is an embroidered version of a true story itself). Will I do the same thing and re-engineer our lives so that a Helen-shaped space is not always so painfully apparent? I surprise myself as I take some paracetamol by saying, "Yes" out very loud to no one but an unmoved Harry the cat. The seeds of change are sown and while I won't be buying a zoo any time soon, I suspect they will grow and flourish more quickly than I or anyone else expects.

For now, though, and in contrast to Matt Damon, I'm touched and grateful and eat and eat (and cat). This includes the 25 assorted specialty pies sent by colleagues who clearly suspect my northern roots. So many in fact that I can't eat or freeze enough and some well-wishers arriving with flowers and food are bemused to find themselves leaving with a complimentary steak and kidney.

A few days later, having vowed that I now need to live forever and must look after myself and lose weight, I peer down at the bathroom scales and see that I've put on nearly half a stone. So much for grief making you fade away.

2.

BINGE THINKING

We are, still, in the seemingly endless period between Helen's death and her funeral and I'm emotionally and physically exhausted. Days are filled with the odious detail of funeral planning and the nights, which should be spent sleeping, find me instead sitting on the sofa binge-watching TV with Harry the cat.

Were it not for the lateness of the hour and the slightly more than sensible amount of red wine I've drunk, it could be a scene from any time in the last 17 years. The big difference is of course Helen's not sitting here with me, nor will she ever do so again. The sheer familiarity of the scene seems to mock my loss so I drink a bit more and give the screen rapt-to-the-point-of-manic attention.

I'm catching up on the dramas that passed me by, such as the brilliant *True Detective* and lots of the documentaries which Helen and the kids never let me watch on the big telly in the lounge because of their perceived boringness.

So it is that at 3:30am and drinking yet another (no. 5) glass of Fleurie, I'm watching my *Dambusters Anniversary*

DVD, discovering the brilliant airmanship of the RAF's 617 Squadron bombing the Ruhr dams in 1943. The benefit of my new-found knowledge of stall-turns under fire is debatable but slumping into sleep on the sofa is eminently preferable to lying awake in a tragically empty bed surrounded on all sides by Helen's belongings. Sinisterly these include her huge bottle of painkilling morphine, the presence of which is a dangerous totem of escape to a grief-drunk widower.

Two occasions in the last week I have found my way to bed at 5am to try and get some sleep before the kids wake up. In the deep stillness of the night I have found myself staring at the bottle, wondering what would happen if I drank what looks like a pint of morphine with a heavy-duty painkiller chaser, of which we have bags full. Would it really offer a version of "To cease upon the midnight with no pain", albeit five hours behind schedule?

I suspect every bereaved person indulges in these morbid thoughts, even if only for a moment, before telling themselves not to be such a selfish wanker.

My conscience, in this case, doesn't have a still small voice but a very strident one that sounds remarkably like my lovely late wife.

Helen: *Don't you dare! What about the kids and your promises to me as I lay dying? Do you think for a second if there was any way I could have chosen to live that I wouldn't have done so? Choose life, go to bed and get more sleep!*

Normal books on bereavement at this point would probably indulge in a well-delivered debate on the sanctity of life and the moral and religious ethics of taking one's own as an escape route from the extremis of grief.

I, however, spent the next few minutes pondering whether my conscience was aware its use of "Choose Life" would evoke in me in a cheery way the phrase written across the T-shirts worn by Wham in "Wake Me Up Before You Go Go". I smile as I hear Helen laughing. It works of course; choosing Wham over Keats, I pour the morphine down the sink with much dilution.

Over breakfast Millie shows she's also feeling the oddness of this waiting time:

Millie: *It's just like the days between Christmas and New Year.*
Matt: *Yep.*
Me: *Nothing's normal, everyone's here and we're all just waiting for it?*

I shudder at this allusion to Helen's funeral but get the point.

Me: *What can we do together which might help?*
Millie: *Look forward to something happy that we'll do after the day. Something Mum would like.*

It's truly terrible that a 14-year-old has to travel this road; death shouldn't even be in her frame of reference. It's too soon.

Later I'm standing in the garden staring into space as

I wait for the salesman to do the recce for a marquee big enough for the guests to have tea in after the funeral. I need the air. Last night I watched the whole first series of *Broadchurch*, finishing at 3:45am, so this morning I look as white, wasted and unshaven as David Tennant's character, DI Alec Hardy.

Thinking about the drama, I'm struck hard by something that Susan Wright, the character played by Pauline Quirke, says when she is forced to reveal her tragic family history:

Susan: *Once death gets its claws into you, it never lets go.*

Looking back at my own life, I got away with it for a long time. My dad died when I was three but I'd no memory of him so was not (psychoanalysts might disagree) impacted by it. By seven, my last surviving grandparent had gone but their deaths had seemed remote. After that I was fortunate to reach my late 40s without incident or upset.

Then suddenly Helen is diagnosed with a villainous cancer, my mother dies, a school friend and contemporary drops dead on a run and our much-loved next-door neighbour succumbs after many years to a fucking cancer she'd kept secret. At her funeral in the local church, Helen beside me, I kept thinking the unthinkable that one day sooner than is right, I would be back there for the worst reason in the world. That day, nine months on, is next week.

I feel that far from being something grim but distant, death is now sitting beside me on life's charabanc. I realise this as Helen's sister Sarah and I go through arrangements for the funeral and none of it is new to me. I have done it all so recently for my mother – the legal niceties, the funeral logistics, catering, order of service etc, all accompanied by ridiculous numbers of copies of her death certificate and a parade of hefty cheques paid out without question or even comment.

Millie and Matt follow me into the garden and start bouncing on the trampoline, much to the surprise of Harry who was lying on it. At 14 and 10, the kids are more than 30 years younger than I was when death got up close and oh so personal. I fear it'll take a lot for the devastating fact of their mother's death not to be the defining moment or ending of their childhood.

I won't let this happen. As Helen lay dying, her body peaceful and her breathing becoming too shallow, I kept talking and talking, being rewarded with gentle squeezes of my hand to let me know she was still there. I did not stop even as her breathing did, as hearing can be one of the last faculties to end, I was told. I was able to tell her so much of what she meant to me and I committed to ensure the kids would grow up to be people she would be proud of, their happiness and growth uncompromised.

I need somehow to push death off the stage and back into the wings for Millie and Matt. A tall order but one that at least shines a beacon for me to head towards through the darkness beyond Helen's "F". That the word "funeral" should ever be prefixed by "Helen's" still seems so wrong; I hate it. I challenge anyone reading this to share for a micro-moment how it feels. Take your living loved one's name and then add "funeral" after it. Feels horrible even knowing it's not true, huh?

Back in the garden Millie suddenly appears beside me and sets our course to a beautifully positive place:

Millie: *Dad, we're not going to be the family known as the one whose mum died. We'll be known for what we achieve – things that she would have been proud of.*
Me: *Wow. OK then.*

My reply is whispered, overwhelmed at her positivity in the face of so much pain.

A car pulls up as the marquee man arrives. He gets out and looks around, assessing the size of the garden, and then walks up to us smiling:

Marquee Man: *So when's the wedding?*

3.

BLACK DAY, BLUE SKY

A live performance of ELO's "Mr Blue Sky" in the church
played by a band of relatives and friends… absolutely
everyone must be invited to the house afterwards. Don't ask
Millie or Matt to do anything – it'll be too much.

I knew that after 17 years of telling me what to do to avoid my screwing up, Helen was giving me her final and most bloody awful set of directions – her wish list for her own funeral.

Sitting at the hospital bedside, her sister Sarah and I listened, both of us in pieces. It jarred so much with Helen's optimism over the past 20 months. But true to form, minutes later she was enthusing about the Italian holiday she'd organised, which was still five months away. As it turned out, she would miss being there by four months and 26 days.

Helen's list was short. It comprised a low-key crematorium committal, followed by a full-fat church celebration of her life. Dying in your 40s means the people who care

are mostly alive and mobile. This would be big and Sarah and I planned a last great hurrah for Helen.

A remarkably good band was formed and a week before the service we asked a few people to turn up and practise. I've been to too many weddings and funerals where the singing is mute or half-hearted – not so for Helen whose vim and vigour in life should be expressed in the congregation's delivery of her last chosen tunes. As it was, about 50 people came to the church. There Sarah, who is very musical, and our more musical close friends, led us through each verse with gusto.

Short of having Jeff Lynne with us it couldn't have been a more beautiful and love-shrouded afternoon, and it was hugely positive for Millie and Matt. It was as if Helen had known that by choosing such a tricky song she would bring us ever closer and create a living, loving "memory box".

All arrangements went well, although my idea to buck tradition and echo our Las Vegas wedding by having the very small number of close family and Annie the nanny travel to the crematorium in a white limo came to nothing.

In the end the fact that we were 10 people was the problem but before that point it had been looking difficult anyway:

Limo Lady: *That postcode is showing a crematorium; is there a church there as well?*
Me: *I don't think so.*
Limo Lady: *Er… so where is the wedding.*

Me: *I didn't say it was a wedding. It's a funeral. My wife's funeral in fact.*

Limo Lady (silence) (more silence): *Sorry but I don't think we can do that date.*

Me: *You didn't ask for the date.*

Limo Lady: *Sorry. (rings off)*

Did they think that grief was going to rub off and embed itself in the upholstery to emerge and deflate the evening for the next prom or hen night hirers? In the end, on the much-dreaded day, the 10 of us headed off in a super luxury little coach with a sensitive grown-up behind the wheel.

My biggest fear had been that the first sight of Helen's coffin would be too much for everyone, so Sarah and I had chosen a beautifully rounded wicker one to lessen its impact.

I held Millie's and Matt's hands so tightly as the hearse arrived with their mother – the woven coffin and its garland of wild flowers not really disguising in any way the full horror of who was in it and why we were there.

We walked behind the ancient Rolls Royce, whose fumes from what was clearly a dangerously over-rich engine added no small amount to the sheer horribleness of the occasion. Later that week I saw it on a recovery truck so I was right and just hope it hadn't broken down "occupied" – it never appeared again in our small town, for which fact I am grateful, so sad are its associations.

We each laid single flowers on Helen – mine a poppy to mark how much she had loved buying a ceramic one from Blood Swept Lands, the Tower of London's centenary Remembrance display. Millie laid a sunflower and Matt a single snowdrop. It was poignant and beautiful as we stood together united in our love for Helen and for one another, protected from despair's worst blows by the emotional chainmail of our linked hearts and hands.

Later, leaving on board our super-coach and fearing a journey of oppressive silence, I had the driver connect my iPod, on which I'd set up a selection of songs that meant something special to Helen, to the vehicle's significant sound system.

As we drove out of the crematorium's gates the driver pressed play and there are still probably people shocked by the group of mourners with "Carry on Screaming!" blaring out of the speakers on their departing coach.

We then returned to town to join the hundreds gathering in the large local church where Helen had been baptised only a few months previously. She had decided to do this as her illness progressed, quietly looking for comfort and strength in all their guises. I think she took more of both from the decision to have Millie and Matt baptised alongside her than the actual fact of it for herself.

Dropping off the others first, the driver and I set off to pick up the flowers from the funeral director to take into the church before driving back. Only as he left did I realise that I'd directed him to the wrong church, one just up the road but far enough when you are carrying a huge and heavy flower arrangement and don't want to be late for your own wife's funeral.

This was another example of "grief haze", where

ostensibly performing well and getting right so much detail one makes a big error that may undo the good stuff.

So like an appalling pastiche of *The Graduate*'s Dustin Hoffman running from the wrong church to the right one, I'm charging down the street with a suspiciously coffin-sized flower arrangement in my arms. The comedy of it at the time was not lost on me even amid the tragedy of it all. Having a wife who could laugh easily and often at life's ironies and ridiculousness is perfect training for bereavement's many hyper-absurdities. Halfway down the road I was tempted to ditch the heavy flowers over a garden wall but somehow it seemed wrong and anyway it would probably have landed on someone, with resultant chaos, or be caught on camera. I kept running.

I'd had no time for nerves until then but as I charged into the church to take my place beside Millie and Matt I was hit suddenly by the weight of responsibility not to screw up; not to fail to do justice to a too-short life so well lived.

When in the past people have referred to funeral services as "celebrations of life" I have been cynical but the new lens which bereavement gives you on so much means this now made total sense. When all is dark, the light of memory shines brighter and is a chance to demonstrate love not loss.

The only one of Helen's wishes we didn't follow in the church was that Millie and Matt insisted on reading Edward Lear's poem, "The Owl and the Pussycat", which we'd held so special for so long and which had been representative to us of our sailing away to Vegas to be married.

They read in turn in front of the 350-400 gathered with such composure, it was the final confirmation that I would be indulging in neither nerves nor breakdown. This wouldn't be the last time that I'd take heart from the kids' youthful version of their mother's determination and courage.

Helen was the star of her show, which is how it should have been, and as I asked the congregation – not sure the vicar approved – to applaud a too-short life so well lived, I could not have meant it more. I always knew I was lucky to have known her but now realise how privileged I was also.

This day was always going to have competition for sheer memorable misery, alongside the day she was diagnosed or when I had to tell the kids almost out of the blue that she would probably die in the next 48 hours. I'd expected this to be the worst but it wasn't even close to either. Instead Helen's wishes had created a perversely beautiful celebration, filled with admiration, salutation and discovery of more than I could ever have guessed about my beautiful and adored wife:

I'll remember you this, I'll remember you this way.

4.

SAD BAD DAD

I wish there were a handbook for newly widowed blokes like me who've been plucked from a fairly stable life stage and lifestyle and thrust unwillingly into the role of sole parent-in-charge of youngish children. There are excellent, frank books about bereavement by Lindsay Nicholson and Lucie Brownlee, and these have helped up to a point, but I am definitely a bloke and carry with that logistical and some would say intellectual disadvantages.

At this point anyone who may recoil at the clichés of parental roles in modern households should skip a page or take a breath and a Valium and read on.

I consider myself – and hopefully was seen – as feminist-friendly but I worked full time and Helen worked part time. It was simply how it panned out financially for reasons that require more space and social engineering insight than I have to hand.

Even so, I had thought myself an enlightened modern male parent, sharing much of Millie and Matt's routine when they were tiny. I was brilliant at nappies as well as the feeds that were biologically possible for me to give.

I have a warm skin temperature and a baby whisperer's abilities to take a crying infant and have them immediately go quiet simply by holding them close. Inevitably, though, in trotting off to work, I never really understood the enormous amount of "stuff" needed to keep our team of four functioning. My competency, judgment and hands-on experience of so much of the daily detail of our lives were therefore lacking, certainly way behind Helen's.

Sure I would do all the usual blokey bins, recycling-type stuff that we men use to pretend hunter-gathering is alive and kicking in safe suburbia. Looking back, though, what I was actually doing was showboating my child-care credentials like a racing driver polishing his winner's trophy without ever recognising the work done by the mechanics who spent all night preparing his car.

Now I realise that as far as the kids and house were concerned, it was never really level pegging but skewed massively towards Helen as primary carer, secondary carer and probably tertiary too, not least in terms of the amount of her head space it must have filled.

With the funeral behind us, I realise that what I need is a route map showing how not to screw things up even if I have to draw my own. People say after bereavement that they won't sweat the small stuff ever again but I disagree, having learned through Helen's illness to value day-to-day detail as the mortar that holds normality in place. Now as a lone parent, normality is what I crave and I hope to sweat buckets of small stuff as we three move forward into the unknown.

But I might have fallen at the first hurdle with Matt

standing before me very upset at the idea of returning to school. It's not simply the horror of Helen's death that's the issue but fear of how other people will react if he has to tell them about it. My fault. The day after her funeral I thought it would help him to go back to cubs.Taking Matt to the church hall in his badge-encrusted shirt and woggle did me some good too. Shovelling him into the car and running late as usual was a ritual done so many times in the happy recent past that it was gloriously comforting.

In true scouting (cubbing) tradition, Akela, the chief, had prepared well in that she'd already told the other cubs and their parents, meaning no child should be too shocked or upset at the fact of Helen's death, and if they were, would have support to hand.

It turned out that the task for the evening was arts and crafts, helped by adult volunteers who'd turn up on the night. All went well, with Matt getting stuck in creating a multi-coloured paper prism, until he finished his work and went proudly to show the adult helper what he'd done.

Helper: *That's lovely, you can take it home to show Mummy tonight.*

Matt wasn't particularly put out at this; compared to the previous few days' turmoil, this was small fry. His reply was in a shrill 10-year-old but matter-of-fact voice:

Matt: *I can't show Mum tonight. It was her funeral yesterday.*

I don't know precisely what the helper's reaction was but I suspect her jaw hit the deck.

So the fallout is that Matt realises people who learn from him about Helen's death will be shocked and react accordingly. Their expressions have upset him, and that has made the prospect of going back to school abhorrent to him in a way it wasn't before.

With Matt calmed down and much happier, I try to work out where his games kit is and know that for the moment my ambitions have become pretty modest – that they go to school on time with the right gear and come home safely to someone in the house, where there's tea to eat and homework to do so that for a moment, if you half close your eyes, it might be as if Helen is simply late home from work. It'll be an illusion but one that might provide comfort for now, not least for me.

Later, sitting at 2am in front of the school website, I have a wobble. The kids' school has a brilliant, supposedly foolproof system where you pre-pay for meals online and the children use their fingerprint to pay for what they eat. It even allows me to see what they've chosen. Looking at the data, I can actually see that right up to the point of Helen's death they were eating well, guzzling paninis and puds right up to the daily limit. How this contrasts to their shrunken appetites over the past days.

Bizarrely, what upsets me more is that I have none of Helen's passwords to top up their nearly empty meal accounts. Maybe because it's food related and so gets to the heart of my role as chief nurturer, or maybe because it's late at night and I've had a drink that I feel almost tearful.

The passwords are a small thing but a clarion call for so much that I don't understand, or didn't know or maybe didn't bother to find out.

Amidst the sense of helplessness I wonder whether I should write a book, "A Sad Dad's Homemaker Guide to the Bleeding Obvious". Any takers?

5.

DEAD WIFE
FINANCIAL STRIFE

I worked in the 1990s for a big life insurance client who at the time ran an advertising campaign, inspired by playwright Dennis Potter's *Pennies From Heaven*. A bad thing would happen, such as serious illness or financial calamity, at which point the music would start and the characters begin to mime and dance along to Nat King Cole's track "There may be trouble ahead...". It was a tricky balance – about 24 seconds of tough news to 36 of dancing to avoid viewers running away from the challenging topics by switching channels.

So it works in my mind's eye late one evening, as, groaning and moaning to an audience of only a bottle of red wine and the cat, I toss down Helen's bank statement, stare into space and don't dance but do start talking to my dead wife:

Me: *I'm screwed! A lifestyle of two salaries and an income of one! How's that going to work?*
Helen (silence of course).

I contemplate the cost of music lessons, grocery shopping, holidays, ballet, mortgage, car and a whole new raft of childcare costs that, with Helen's death, will now come out of one salary.

What about our own life insurance? Looking again at the list of outgoings, I wonder how I, of all people, could have ended up underinsured. Back in the day, researching testimonials for my clients, I'd really seen the danger of not having insurance protection for the worst that life can send your way. That we had any cover at all was thanks to some helpful on-the-road lessons from bit-of-a-geezer Barry who was a top and very wealthy salesman.

One morning I travelled with Barry to see his clients.

Me: *In research groups people don't talk about death – particularly their own. Is it different in practice in real life?*

Barry: *No – probably worse because they also don't want to pay premiums when they are well, have lots of other outgoings and think they are immortal anyway.*

Me: *So how do you do it?*

Barry: *You've gotta reverse the hearse up to their front door and let them smell the flowers on the coffin!*

The form this took was to get a husband and wife to both fill in estimates of how much money would be needed if the wife/mother died. Almost always, the husband would call it ridiculously low and his wife would be spot on.

During the row that followed, no selling at all was required by Barry, the chastened couple snapping up the life policy he placed before them.

However sharp-edged Barry's practice might seem, if the worst happened then the survivor would be back embracing and thanking him.

The problem with developing these ads was always that one couldn't make a life-changing event too dreadful, as absolute grief would be the problem at that moment, not money. We believed that it would take ages after a loved one's death for the issue of money to creep up the list of priorities. We were very wrong; I now know only too well, thanks to fucking cancer and its dreadful works.

I've learned that the time between the death of a loved one and the first fear for the financial future barely leaves time for the last note of the final hymn to fade at the funeral. Despite my knowing the devils of under-insurance, helped by Barry's spiv-edged master class, I'd had the usual denial and lack of interest, fear and avoidance of acknowledging death and planning for it. It meant that Helen and I were far from well covered. I take another deep gulp of the Barolo (an indulgence whose days may be numbered) and ramble on aloud and pitiful but unheard by anyone who cares.

Me: *Better me. Better me to have died and Helen lived. Millie and Matt would have a mum and Helen would have banked a ton of cash. So wrong.*

It's true financially the payout would be massively bolstered because unlike Helen's job, mine came with a generous death-in-service benefit. Millie and Matt would have no dad, but would be at least equally loved and have no money worries going into and through university – especially if Helen went on to remarry. We'd joked about this when making our will so long ago, despite thinking that we were immortal:

Me: *You'll find me hard to replace without spending some cash on yourself.*
Helen (feigning puzzlement): *How so?*
Me: *To find a new husband you'll need all the help you can get – new clothes, a sports car, boob job and maybe some liposuction.*
Helen: *Cheeky sod!* (throwing hefty draft of will at me).

That seems a lifetime ago – in fact it was quite literally Helen's lifetime ago. Now, looking miserably at her finances, things are not looking better with the passage of time or wine. Pretty much all Helen's salary went on childcare, proving in silent witness how much she loved her job.

It comes home to me that our brilliant nanny, Annie, who has been with us for 10 years and allowed us both to work and whom I'm aware Millie and Matt need more than ever, requires getting on for a quarter of my salary for four days a week. Gosh.

This is sustainable if I keep my job and income stable but therein lies the bit no one ever, and I really mean EVER, mentions when one is doing financial planning. My job means travelling regularly and how sustainable is that with two children who are already showing signs of hating me being away and simmering with anxiety that something else bad will happen? I might need to work less intensely or not at all for a while. Also, if I am honest with myself, can I ever be bothered again to have the same level of dedication to anything that takes me away from the kids? The old ad's strapline *"For the life you don't yet know"* turns out to have been a belter – I had not a clue of any of this. Trouble ahead financially but surely after all that's happened money isn't going to make us a happy family again.

I'd had enough to drink to answer out loud my own question:

Me: *Yeah, money doesn't make you happy but bugger me it helps.*

Breaking down the fourth wall of the book for a moment with good reason, I'd like to say I'm not a financial adviser but consider yourselves now nagged – check and improve your life cover now.

So if, heaven forbid, the worst happens, you can raise your own glass to me because it won't be money worries that stop you dancing.

6.

Not Working, Sheryl

In the meantime, I have to pretend that the world isn't totally shit by returning to work, and I'm worried. Since Helen's funeral, I've been digging out a routine for Millie and Matt from the rubble of a domestic happiness all but flattened by their mother's death.

It's not my employers who are the problem – they have been great as they were throughout Helen's illness, when I'd continued to do the trips abroad but when in the UK would rarely be expected to go into the office.

Nor do I dread going in because I think everyone will be watching me – very few colleagues know that Helen is dead. From Helen's bedside, I'd lobbied human resources' Ivan for the news of her death to be kept quiet. Ivan had been as good as his word, while also warning me of the dangers of keeping shtum – that people wouldn't cut me any slack if my performance was poor, and might be insensitive to the rawness of it all for me. I would need a very thick skin.

Fair warning, but a rhino hide seems a reasonable trade-off for being spared the awkwardness of "I'm so sorry..." exchanges and to avoid seeing the fear in people's eyes that I might blub like a baby.

Yet I fear disaster. They say the routine of work provides stability for the bereaved – this includes Facebook executive Sheryl Sandberg, who returned to work 10 days after her husband's unexpected death. I respect so much of what she has written but, God, she must love her job – for me there's been a distinct recalibration in what I give a toss about, which does not include some of the pain, politics and occasional arse-covering required for success in my media-related industry.

It might be easier were I a doctor, whose degree of importance in saving lives would meet my narrower definition of what now matters.

There were signs, even from the morning of Helen's death, that the tectonic plates of my worldview had shifted. It was 7am and I was en route back from the hospital to be home when Millie and Matt woke.

Emotionally empty and physically exhausted after a long night in Helen's room saying farewell, I needed to bolster myself before telling the kids that their mum had died. Seeing a coffee shop open as I entered town, I'd pulled over for an Americano.

A few minutes later I was parked on the High Street outside the bank sprawled across the car's back seat with my coffee, the privacy glass of the rear windows making me invisible to the world.

An Audi sports car pulled up sharply and, leaving his engine running and door open, a suited figure of about 35 emerged and put his card into the nearest cashpoint.

Minutes passed and, despite it being so early, he had a meltdown that would shame a toddler, albeit with language that was more naval than nursery:

Audi Man: *Fuck, fuck, fuck, fuck, fuuuuck!*

From nowhere I was consumed by burning anger. That he should behave that way for so small an inconvenience. In a mad departure from law-abiding etiquette, I wanted to jump in and steal his smart-arse car. That would really have given him something to swear about, as I found out how well that big engine put the rubber on the road.

I didn't break the law but could so easily have done as never before. The moment passed, he drove off and I was seemingly still fit to be a member of middleish England.

Fate, however, had not finished with me. From around the corner came a much older man, furtive and conspicuous; a present-day version of George Cole's Flash Harry from the St Trinian's films, peering up and down the empty road. He stopped before the cashpoint only four feet from my hidden vantage point. Seeing no one about, he started to remove something from its surround. I was stunned. It was a sting in which the potty-mouthed Audi man's cash card had been cloned.

The previous day, I would have been photographing this scene, calling the police or even wading in, but today – and maybe forever – I didn't give a toss.

What this means for my work I'm not yet sure, but it's likely to be trickier than I imagined – my view of the world has shifted from compliance (with an occasional wildcard moment) to something much more intolerant of my time and life being wasted by stuff that just doesn't matter.

If only I'd pleased my mum and become a surgeon it might all be so much easier.

7.

THE GILDED CAGE

Ruth, my kind and unflappable bereavement counsellor is looking a little "flappy". Tall, in her 50s,
with grown-up kids and a gentle, reassuring manner, our
conversation over the past hour has had her struggling to
believe her ears and not slop her coffee.

Ruth (with quiet concern): *So Adam, how have things been?*
Me: *This morning I came downstairs and the cat had turned
yellow.*

I throw it out there mischievously but it is all too true. I
came down to breakfast to find Harry, Helen's large white
Siberian cat, was bright yellow. I did as one always does
with the impossible and shut my eyes a moment and tried
again.

Running my hand down his back made my fingers look
like mini bananas as a bell rang in my memory of Helen
annoyed after brushing the sleeve of her favourite cream
jacket on some lilies in the hall of a friend's house and

finding it stained the same bright yellow. Sure enough, there on the table were lilies a well-wisher must have sent the day before and someone had placed in a vase on the kitchen table. Harry, like his late mistress and with more relish, I suspect, had been rubbing himself against them all night.

The bell in my head rang again as a fact stored long ago about lilies being poisonous to cats was retrieved and quickly confirmed online. Cats lick it off and it poisons them. Harry seemed fine and calm or at least was so until I picked him up and ran him upstairs and into the bath, shampooing away his yellow highlights. He is a gentle soul and didn't use his claws at all, although one could sense his displeasure by the "stood on tail" volume of his wailing woe.

It was not yet 8am and the day had started with the sort of unpredictable angst and humour that was beginning to characterise our version of bereavement.

Millie and Matt come down dressed for school.

Millie: *Why is Harry wet?*
Me: *I washed him!*
Matt (distractedly): *Why?*
Me: *He turned yellow from the poisonous lily pollen.*
Matt (panicking): *Oh is he all right. Is he all right?*
Me: *He seems fine but I'll work from home and keep an eye on him today.*
Matt (still anxious): *Don't let him out of your sight, Dad. Please!*
Millie: *Why did you let Harry near the lilies, Dad?*

Matt: *Is breakfast ready? I need to leave soon.*
Millie: *Is my PE kit washed?*

Our new life is laid bare. The kids fear loss more than before and in particular about Harry, who was their mother's adored pet. On top of which the assumption that I can work from home when needed is already there since I have been so present of late.

Obviously being a parent means that such dramas which are my fault, i.e. all of them, will not get in the way of my doing the basics of cooking, cleaning and generally organising things.

Hearing this gives Ruth a break and she grasps the more familiar topic that doesn't involve a yellow cat:

Ruth: *You are now sole parent in charge and the rock on which they are rebuilding their sense of a normal life. It means you carry the load not just because they don't do stuff to help at home but also it's a sort of test that with your wife gone things can be close to how they were or are with their friends' families.*
Me: *For how long? Forever?*
Ruth: *Probably not. It'll take time for them to separate what matters and what doesn't so much. For now though it means doing nearly everything that matters to them or at least everything you can manage without keeling over. Yellow cats included. You could ask them to do a bit more to help with the basic chores though.*
Me: *I get that. In time they'll do more chores but not yet – I don't think they should suddenly have to do jobs they*

didn't previously just because their mum died. It's hard enough.

Ruth: *It would take the pressure off you though.*

Me: *Yeah, but it's not their fault Helen died. Maybe when they're older. I do feel some stress though about what people think – that I need to be seen to be coping with no balls dropped.*

Ruth: *Does it matter what other people think?*

Me: *Not so much about the small things… but what happens if I sell the house, buy a Ferrari or am seen cavorting in the hot tub with a swimsuit model? Am I locked into a role others expect of me for the next eight years until Matt leaves home? A gilded cage but with black bunting!*

OK, so this was a stretch. Swimsuit models were never lining up for my attention or hot tub when I was single/younger/less emotionally battered and actually it's an old, plumbed-in Victorian roll-top bath in the garden.

However, I was dramatising for impact, such is my alarm at my emerging status as widower of the parish. Where I live is pretty prosperous and families with children are the norm. Crossing the road, you play "Frogger" between Ocado deliveries and seven-seat Volvos. Sure, there are divorces and deaths but being single with kids makes me stand out.

Add the tragedy of it being death, not divorce, that has created one's single status and the spotlight shines brighter. Overlay then the death of one's wife and the status of widower is akin to being a lighthouse on a dark night that someone has stuck a Roman candle up.

I feel, as never before, a sense of visibility and vulnerability. As a family we're in danger of being defined by Helen's death, our loss becoming public property like a pregnant woman's bump seems to be. Don't get me wrong, people have been so very kind and supportive, and their love helped me avoid the whisky-until-you-forget route in the early days.

However, I now get a sense that everything I do is viewed as a conspicuous extension of Helen's life-limiting illness and early death – against which my behaviour will be deemed appropriate or not. It's as if there's a script of behaviours for the bereaved, the "Miss Havisham" rules. This comprises a set of unwritten and therefore unchallengeable edicts to govern my new, unwanted, unvalued widower status. I am pretty sure that not only do these rules not include much merriment, they almost certainly involve a long period in the wilderness where pretty much anything that is not a linear progression of a middle-England version of Victorian mourning will be frowned upon.

I'm not saying that I feel there's a Greek chorus looking on who think they have a right and remit to critique my behaviour but… sorry, yes, that's exactly how I feel. Not everyone by any means, and not the obvious candidates, but some for sure.

This challenges my screaming desire to seize life by the lapels and behave if not badly then unexpectedly. Why would I try to live out the same life I would have had with Helen, just a more miserable, lonely and unfulfilled version of it? It's not what she would want, nor what

Millie and Matt will need. For the moment, what matters is stability and sweating the small stuff until things have settled down, but change will – and should – come.

My lovely divorced friend, Jo, who has been by herself for years with her two boys, brought home to me the fact that being sole grown-up-in-charge means things can happen very fast:

Jo: *Being the only adult in the house frees you to make decisions and move quickly if you want to – faster indeed than people around you are used to, or can sometimes accept. It can make you a talking point.*

I obviously would never have chosen to be alone but I see the power it brings – a not unattractive freedom to make quick, big decisions that will carry the kids away from their grief by creating a new life – not just the old one without Mum.

So bereavement is empowering me to deal with bereavement, which is an unexpected and morbidly virtuous circle.

Across on the sofa, Ruth's silence after my clumsy hot tub point is now deafening. Seeing her adrift in a sea of uncertainty, I throw her a lifebelt:

Me: *Ruth, by any chance are most of the people you visit a lot older than me?*

Ruth (with a warm, wry smile): *Much older and usually women. For widows in their 80s, the topic of swimsuit models in hot tubs is not as common as one might think…*

Our conversation has thrown up some big issues, which lie unresolved on the table for later. This amateur counselling is proving to be of greater value than I suspected in getting my issues of angst to declare themselves. More professional help to resolve them may be a good idea in the future.

Not just yet, though, with cats to wash, breakfasts to make and a thousand as yet unknown incoming issues in the wings. Actually a Miss Havisham lifestyle looks not so bad suddenly – she had staff so had it easy.

8.

MINDFULNESS SHMINDFULNESS

Were I ever to be asked to shortlist the most influential people in my life, John the long-serving barman of the boozer in my northern hometown would be right up there.

Called to the bar at a young age, he's spent a lifetime earning the means serving behind it to drink endlessly at it. In many ways he is a perfect "just in time" supply model. His appearance is consistent with 40 years dedicated to a life seen and lived through the bottom of a glass. This has given him the complexion of a hill farmer whose protection against the elements ended long ago when his bothy blew down.

In many ways, the most unsettling of his traits for the unwary is that his rolling, unfocused eyes are perfect accompaniments to a husky drinker's croak that intersperses his still relatively effective bartending with the mutterings of his bitter subconscious.

He'll shout:

"What can I get you?" *but mutter,* "A good kicking".

"Pint of Landlord, sir?" *with the less audible rider* "... right up your arse".

It is unclear whether he knows that his conscious mind's words come with a chaser from his inner monologue but one suspects not. All this is more than fine. He was never destined to be an action standard to his clientele of sobriety, health and sanity; you'll understand, then, that ever since I discovered we were born in the same year when the 60s still swung, the worse he looks the better I feel about myself.

I'm pleased to remark that the last time I travelled north my brilliant anti-hero John looked like absolute crap. Close childhood friend and alehouse-familiar Pete has a view on this schadenfreude as he does on most things:

Me: *Not sure he's the best reference for a fitness buddy!*
Pete: *Ah It's the Fonz factor.*
Me (sighing): *Remind me...*
Pete: *The Fonz looked cool because he hung out in Al's diner with Potsie and Ralph. If he'd turned up with James Dean and Marlon Brando, he'd have looked like a short-arsed prick.*
Me: *I remember that now – Viz circa 20 years ago!*
Pete: *I never said it was my theory.*

Times have changed though since Helen's funeral:

Me: *Looking a bit better than him isn't really enough now – the kids don't need a fat, unhealthy dad likely*

to drop dead on them.
Pete: *You're not quite that unhealthy!*

Pete's reassurance and tactical use of "quite" was, I noticed, accompanied by a pointed look down at the bit of weight that comfort and kindness food had added in the weeks since Helen died. I parked the issue there but it would need to be addressed in future – I needed to be well, to do everything I could to live and definitely not die or be seriously ill, at least until the kids have "flown". Ideally longer, frankly.

As it was, this food for thought was eaten sooner than expected. When I next pilgrimage north to visit relatives, John is not behind the bar and hasn't been for some time. His well-worn path, weaving across the busy road from the pub where he worked and drank to the one in which he drank even more, has caught him out, and it's not looking good for his return.

Hearing this has brought to me more powerfully than Pete's cheeky glance at my muffin top (maybe should be pie crust) that since Helen died I have not been looking after myself. I have yet to go to bed before 2am or entirely sober. The half bottle a day of red wine I've been slurping ("half" spelled W-H-O-L-E), plus whisky and the assortment of carbs delivered by well-wishers have seen my head spin and weight climb. And so I start running.

I used to love running. I would put in enough distance to give me a "get out of jail card" to eat what I liked. I used to run marathons but stopped when Helen, Millie, Matt and I started karate (or at least the kids did and we took to training with them as encouragement and support).

Putting on the trainers feels like coming home and the first few runs remind me not only what I've been missing but also just how unfit I now am. I pant like Ivor the Engine facing a steep Welsh viaduct with a leaky boiler.

Should I really be reaching 180 beats per minute? No! A rule-of-thumb maximum of 220bpm minus your age would have me at 40 years old which I waved goodbye to long ago. I book in to see our local GP and get a check-up as I can't risk ending up face down in a puddle. I'm still haunted by the fact that a school friend my age died on a run of a heart attack despite being very fit – a pre-existing heart condition was later revealed, although that is no consolation to his wife and three kids. I need to make sure I am building my fitness on robust foundations.

However, going into the surgery brings a grief ambush as I recall so many medical appointments with an ever more ill Helen. A very dark cloud descends. It's simply too soon to be doing this, so I cancel the appointment and scuttle off.

It seems that the subject of my mental wellbeing is on a wider agenda. Someone at work appears to have nominated me for a bloody mindfulness course.

Is it because there's something in my behaviour or performance that's worrying those few colleagues who know about Helen's death? I've been back only a short time but I thought I'd made a good show of things – I say "show" as what lies beneath is definitely less commitment and respect for my job's importance. So I check out who else is going to the six workshops. Pleasingly, it's a broad cross-section of colleagues who as a group do not look like the collection of emotionally strung-out, hollow-eyed, hand-wringing lost souls that I'd feared I'd be matched with.

I see that blunt, bearded Roger, a straight-talking colleague from Otley, is going too, so ask him:

Me: *Why do you think you've been put up for the course?*
Roger: *God knows – I've got no time to waste on a load of bull. It's probably to help them win a "great places to work" nomination. I don't need a mindfullofshit course now or ever. It's not like anyone's dying or got cancer.*

I smile thinly. Roger's words rub salt, pepper and chilli oil into the bloody maw of my emotions. It was right to tell so few colleagues of Helen's death from cancer but it doesn't insulate me from this sort of unintended verbal evisceration.

But I do feel better about the course. In fact, I start to think mindfulness might help. I'd embraced Eckhart Tolle's thinking some time before the word itself became a badge of trendy self-awareness. Living in the "now" and suppressing my "inner monologue" had helped me to live alongside Helen's illness for nearly two years. During those difficult yet rich months, I hadn't wished to look towards an uncertain future and it had been too painful to look back to times before her deadly diagnosis.

My understanding of mindfulness is still summed up by the homily:

"The past is history, the future's a mystery but today is a gift – that's why it's called the present."

These words, hopefully based on some ancient maxim, are spoken by the truly wise Master Oogway in *Kung Fu Panda*. OK, he's a fictional tortoise but has probably done more to shout out the philosophy than any unwilling participants in corporate training.

So, reading the course-joining questionnaire, my eyes widen when it asks:

Course Guidance: *In the past 12 months have you experienced anything that could be termed stressful?*

Ouch. I e-mail back:

Me: *Mother died, new job, child scarred by barbed wire, wife died.*

I suspect this reply will be as welcome on someone's screen as a pile of well-rotted manure. Sure enough, within minutes the phone rings and a gentle female voice comes on. It's Lucia from the training company; she's speaking in a tone you'd use to a man whose heels were the only contact point with the ledge around the top of a very tall building. In what follows I do my best to sound calm and well balanced:

Lucia: *Hello, it's Lucia from the training team.*

Me: *Hi Lucia, I'm guessing it's about my reply.*

Lucia: *Yes. To be honest I don't think it appropriate for you to come on the course. With your level of stress it might just tip you over into a darker place.*

Me: *Hold on. Darker than what? I actually hoped it might help – help me deal with embracing the daily normality of family and corporate life…*

Lucia (soothing and smoothing away): *Mindfulness can do that but sitting in a circle with others whose biggest stress is that their Ocado order never gets delivered in the timeslot they've booked may provoke some deep emotion that won't help you.*

Me: *What you mean is that it won't help you run a course if one of the participants breaks down or beats the hapless online grocery shopper to a pulp with his own A4 pad.*

Lucia: *Not at all. It's our concern for you.*

Me: *If so why not try to help me? Make me the poster boy for the power of mindfulness as I move on undefined by past tragedy and undaunted by the future.*

She has no answer. I let it pass and withdraw.

"Their loss not mine," I tell myself to cover my surprisingly sharp sense of rejection. I repeat the phrase later to Jo, my single-mother friend, with an arrogance born of pique.

The truth remains that I do believe in the "power of now" as expressed not by trainers but long ago by a terminally ill Dennis Potter in an interview with Melvyn Bragg on Channel 4:

Potter: *But the nowness of everything is absolutely wondrous ... you have to experience it... the glory of it, if you like, the comfort of it, the reassurance... not that I'm interested in reassuring people – bugger that. The fact is, if you see the present tense, boy do you see it! And boy can you celebrate it.*

In the darkest days around Helen's diagnosis and then death I could never have imagined I'd be able to celebrate the beauty of the world around me again, yet I can, maybe even more so. The world is the same but I am not. Grief has changed me. The emerging question is, "to what?"

9.

WAY to Go

There are opportunities you never welcome – the letter from the police offering you the chance to go on a speed awareness course, an illustrated guide to better lovemaking from one's partner or, as I now have, the chance to join a club exclusively for people who've experienced the screaming pain of close bereavement.

Widowed & Young (WAY) is a support group with more than 2500 members. It embraces everyone, whether married or not, with or without kids and whatever your sexual orientation – as long as you're 50 or under when bereaved. They know full well you'd rather be anywhere else:

WAY: *We're sorry you're eligible to join us, but we're glad you found us.*

Surprisingly, so am I, as it turns out but maybe not entirely for reasons that they might have foreseen or even approve.

I'd heard about WAY from Lucie Brownlee's book, which paints a warts-and-all but positive description of some of the people she met and the help she'd found there. So far I'd steered clear of it, though for much the same reasons as I'd ducked my friend Laura's well-meaning suggestion:

Laura: *Adam, I have a friend whose wife died three years ago. It might help you to meet him.*
Me: *You know, I'm not sure that I'm ready for that yet* **(thinking: nor ever will be while there's breath left in my body).**

This instinct to avoid immersing myself in someone's else tragedy is a biggie.

I need to be lifted out of my slough of despond, not to join others wallowing in it. It's why I wonder how online dating sites for widows and widowers work – over dinner do you talk about funerals, memorials, crematorium horrors, embalming and bereavement benefits? Chances of hanky panky at the end of such an evening = sub-zero. Chances of hanky wiping away tears from eyes = certain. Probably not my tears, though, as I've yet to cry; I haven't done so since the day of Helen's diagnosis. This is not for want of the pain of grief; and it worries me hugely that my dry-eyed façade might be taken as such an omission by everyone around me. I cry long and disconsolately inside. But externally – with real live wet tears – I just can't do it.

My powerful abhorrence of mingling with mourning is given no truck by my cousin Holly who is a cliché of gloriously brassy northernness. She's a massive and particularly loud advocate of WAY. Her best friend's husband died and his widow is a WAY cheerleader and active organiser.

Holly: *Come on, give WAY a chance. Do you realise how arrogant it sounds when you say you're fine? You can't be!*

Me: *No chance. I'm not a clubby sort of bloke and I'm not going to start now.*

In the 30 years I've been a member of my classic car club I've only been to one meeting. There were too many people fond of cleaning their bumpers with a toothbrush to bother with social discourse or personal hygiene. I don't do clubs.

Holly (clearly thinks being family = being given a God-given right to frankness which is borderline rude): *You are being so childish!*

Me: *I'm not talking to strangers about Helen's death now or ever. Would you?*

Holly doesn't let me off the hook.

Holly: *I'm not deep grieving – you are. For Christ's sake what have you got to lose? You might even discover there are people who worry every day that they're going crackers, just like you do!*

Me (with a whiff of anger): *Stop!*

Holly (laughing): *Anyway, you old fooker, how many clubs do you think exist in which you still qualify as young? Not many, bonnie lad!*

I smile. Holly is not that much younger than me and her voice is laden with good intent. To be fair she has a point – not so much about the age thing, although it is true but I've been looking for an explanation for my strange, aka a bit crazy, behaviour.

In the weeks since Helen's death, I've developed an hour-long nightly bedroom ritual. I find myself picking up objects that were Helen's – her diary, her hairbrush with blond hairs still attached, her makeup and even her dressing gown – and then spend ages trying to place them exactly as she had last touched them. I know it has something to do with maintaining a close connection but it also smacks of bereavement-induced OCD.

It always happens at 1am, adding further to my exhaustion and giving it a sense of the macabre that only the hours of deep darkness can imbue. To overlay even more weirdness I know that as long as I jump into my tragically empty bed by 2am I'll be asleep in minutes. However, if I miss the 2am slot even by a minute I can lie awake for hours wondering what the bloody hell has happened to our lives.

So I have bowed, indeed bent, to Holly's tungsten will and joined WAY; paying my sub and waiting a few days due to the quaint fact that my confirmation of membership comes by post. A hint perhaps already that time is less important in this transaction than the texture of how it feels to be in a club whose entry qualifications are about as miserable as you can get.

A few days later my membership arrives, which will let me access the forums and member profiles. As the clock ticks past 2am and a long night of lying awake and alone beckons, I sit down in front of my Mac to write my profile.

Putting as little of myself as possible into it – when Helen died/what of – away I go.

It's a revelation. There are no fewer than nine members within three miles of me, including three widowers. The majority of profiles have descriptions as brief as my own and most deaths are also from fucking cancer. All of which is unexpected but actually very comforting – I am really not alone, even locally.

Roaming the forums, I find people who have many of the same grief issues and experiences as I do and who are being supported by the instinctive good sense of other travellers. Somehow I had expected it to be deadly depressing and it is that and a whole lot more. Luckily the more in this case is that it's the one group in which when someone says that they understand, they really do and that matters more than anything.

I'm humbled by the trauma of some of those whose loved ones have gone more brutally and suddenly than I experienced with Helen. It is like some morbid Top Trumps that you don't want to win, although we all ended up at a graveside.

There is something else, though. A sudden thought, the clarity and brutality of which punches me hard on the nose. Ignoring that it is now 3am and with social etiquette diluted by drink, I call Holly's mobile knowing that she sleeps closer to it than she does her partner. It rings six times...

Holly: *Adam? Is everything all right?*

Me: *Everyone's fine.*

Holly: *So what the bloody hell...?*

Me: *I said everyone's fine not everything's fine.*

Holly: *What!* (exhales then more gently)... *so what's up?*

Me: *I joined WAY like you said!*

Holly: *Well done, pet.*

Me: *It's made me understand that there are people who are coping, who have had worse bereavements than mine and yet are still standing. It's what I needed to know.*

Holly: *That's great – Whehay for WAY. It's what I hoped you'd think. So what's the problem?*

Me: *There are people who've been there for years who are still talking as if their partner died yesterday – bereavement's defining their lives. It's so depressing.*

Holly: *As your mum would say "Let Isaac worry" – for now get some sleep and get on top of it tomorrow. Night night.*

She's right, I guess, although with no disrespect to them it still troubles me to have so many bereaved people so active in the group but still so sad after years. WAY obviously supports that long-term need but it's not a happy destination for me nor one I want to accept – starting now.

This fight back starts the next bedtime when I slip between the sheets late but earlier than usual and without the spooky tragi-ritual with Helen's things. I remind myself that I need sleep to be in the best shape for Millie and Matt – they are the true reminders of Helen, not a hairbrush or comb.

I also go on a spree of clearing our bedroom to bin/

loft/charity. There's a very bad moment finding Helen's reading glasses. These were so much a feature of her appearance that knowing there's no longer a face to place them on is an unexpected and painful emotional ambush. Team WAY will be nodding reading this. They get it.

This scorched-earth clearance strategy works and I'm stronger – another small notch forward on this dreadful journey. *"I don't want to belong to any club that will accept people like me as a member"* – Groucho Marks was wrong. Way to go, WAY.

Check out WAY if you have been bereaved and qualify. It has a sister organisation for people in their 50s and 60s, called Way Up, which I assume is not just for people in Yorkshire despite the way it sounds spoken aloud.

10.

No Way OK

Well Meaning Friend (WMF): *How are you doing, Adam?*
Me: *I'm OK, thanks.*

So the conversation goes with everyone I haven't seen for what feels like only five minutes. Believe me, this isn't a problem. I love that people care enough to help me face the grief-based challenges of single parenthood. It's just that as the weeks roll on since Helen's death, I'm answering, "OK", while thinking:

Me: *How the buggery bollocks do I know?*

The word "OK" is itself chosen with care. It is a positive response without overblowing it. Being *"Bloody brilliant"* would be much too perky for someone whose wife has died. A shame as it is possible for the bereaved to have the odd nano-second of true joy fuelled by too much beer, a cheery friend or a YouTube video of a cat running around with its head wedged in an empty box of Lucky Charms.

If I avoid replies that are extremely positive even if true, I definitely also avoid sharing the extreme negatives when I'm feeling miserable. Otherwise this might go:

WMF: *How are you doing, Adam?*
Me: *Dreadfully! I'm so low that I sometimes wonder whether it would be easier to pack my pockets with tins of cat food and jump off the end of the bloody pier…*

…sort of thing.

This reply is not that bad and outranks "OK" in accuracy but would still be guaranteed to have the other party, often asking out of polite concern, scurrying away faster than the proverbial rat out of the aqueduct. People's fear that they might be the person closest to me when the music stops and I break down big time in tears is palpable. It's a sort of nervousness-of-what-might happen-but-probably-won't that means theatre goers avoid the front three rows at the pantomime lest they are called on stage to become the hapless butt of some festive comedy.

Mischievously, I'm tempted to turn on the tears just to see what happens but have avoided doing so with stern lectures to my humour-hungry self that people are only ever trying to help so not to mess with their heads.

Also I still can't cry, so they should have no fear of my tears. I cope and never ever blub. I worry that not doing so removes from Millie and Matt a sense of permission that it is OK for them to cry. So I compensate in other, often heavy-handed ways of giving them a chance to cry for their mum. Some ideas, like visits to her favourite places, have worked and others, like counselling, have manifestly failed.

Even getting Millie and Matt in the same room as the bereavement counsellor has been difficult, as they've come at me with a brutal logic tinged with outrage that I should think that they need it.

Me: *His job is to listen and maybe help you think and talk about things that have been left unsaid.*

Matt: *Did he know Mum?*

Me: *No, but that doesn't matter. It's his job to get to know you.*

Millie: *So you're paying him?*

Me: *Yes. This is what he does every day for families like ours to help them.*

Matt: *Helps them do what?*

Me: *Deal with grief and loss so that it doesn't cause problems in the future.*

Matt: *It's causing me problems now. I don't want to talk to a stranger about Mum. I deal with it myself.*

Me (slightly exasperated): *It's the right thing to do.*

M and M: *We're not going!*

In the end I'd got special leave from Mr Henman and Ms Fisher, the ever-kind headteachers of the kids' sensitive and supportive schools for them to take time out for family counselling. It was this pseudo-endorsement by school that swung it and so we found ourselves sitting in an over-heated room with genial, softly spoken Danish counsellor, Per.

We sat, Millie to Per's left by a large fan that blew hot air in everyone's faces, Matt to his right and me opposite. An hour later the dialogue split was pretty much:

Adam: 10%
Millie: 5%
Per: 20%
Matt: 65%

Like a boxer moving effortlessly around the ring, Matt had parried every one of Per's gentle probes by using it as a springboard to move the conversation in a new direction, so leaving behind the original question.

Per: *Do you think you talk enough about your mother?*
Matt: *We'd usually call her "mum".*
Per: *Do you think you talk enough about your mum?*
Matt: *What would you call enough?*
Per: *You tell me maybe.*
Matt: *How do I know what's enough?*

By the end the very act of being there and talking probably helped Matt, and I think Per felt that things had gone well. I had suggested previously that Matt was a greater concern to me than Millie; usually bottling things up to self-medicate, his grief taking a different shape to that of his sister, who wore her emotions as openly as her mother.

The session ended with Per smiling at Matt, speaking words of gentle encouragement:

Per: *Well, that wasn't so bad, was it, Matt? Not like going to the dentist!*

Matt (with casual, easy charm): *Actually I like my dentist.*

Per looked pained and noticeably didn't push too hard for a rematch.

Afterwards I asked Millie why she had been so quiet.

Millie: *He had such a quiet voice and the fan was so loud that I couldn't hear him. Can we not go again, please, Dad?*

So we didn't. Bad decision maybe but like a first aider who, confronted with a number of casualties, heads to help the quiet ones first, I take heart that their vocal objections to counselling may just mean they don't need it.

I realise that we had been there as much for my benefit as theirs. I had enjoyed the "time out" and am still haunted by my mother's lack of counselling in the 1960s after my dad died, which hit her hard in later life. Hence she ended it with too much alcohol and not enough joy, with only early onset Alzheimer's blunting the sense of loss.

Day to day the fact that I never cry remains a morose fixation – a harbinger for future problems perhaps. My lack of tears contradicts much "grief literature" which sees the bereaved in floods of tears while barely coping, often for years. I need proper counselling – lack of tears I know is not lack of love for Helen but what does it mean? I need help beyond the tea, sympathy and friendship of the local church, welcome and kind though Ruth is.

Maybe my tears will come in torrents when our lives have reached a more structured new order, although now that may not be for a while yet. Even I as was thinking this, that the pieces of the jigsaw might just start to be assembled to match the picture on a box that has me, Millie, Matt and just the memory of Helen on it, they've been sent flying up again in all directions. Annie, our nanny, who has been with us for as long as Matt can remember, has announced that she is pregnant with her first child.

This is fantastic news and Helen would have been as delighted as I am but it means major change whether or not she comes back. I have a bit of time but I need to look towards coping without Annie at a practical level and, more pertinently, at an emotional level, as she is, in 10-year-old Matt's straight talking:

Matt: *Not my mum, but the closest I've got because I see more of her than any woman alive.*

Her news also demonstrated that people sometimes don't know how to react to bereavement and may unintentionally be outrageously hurtful. The winner so far is Dick (not his real name).

Me: *I'm dreading telling the kids yet again that the main woman in their lives is not going to be around. Great news for Annie but a bummer for the kids.*
Dick: *When's she off?*
Me: *Back end of the year but I should tell them asap.*

Dick looks thoughtful then smirks:

Dick: *She must have conceived pretty much around the time Helen died. You weren't taking comfort in the arms of your nanny, were you? Eh, mate?*

Me (wide-eyed): *Meaning...*

Dick: *That... that...*

Me: *You do know that it's me you're talking to, not the other school dads down the pub?*

Dick: *Er... no, no... yes... sorry that came out all wrong. I mean... er... er... I didn't mean...*

The urge to break the karate oath and kick his balls round the walls was powerful but fleeting. I saw at once in his eyes the full horror of the realisation that he'd not said this about me but to me, and so let it go.

That I can now tolerate this level of unthinking crassness indicates a new understanding of how ill-equipped many people are to deal with the bereaved. They stay silent, avoid you or simply panic and talk bollocks whenever the conversation strays bereavementwards.

It's just another step in my assimilation back into the community in my new, totally alien role, as widower parent. I've already become used to being the honorary "mum" at Matt's primary school. The high/low point was attending the parents' evening to hear in detail the sex education Matt would receive.

Held in the early evening, it might have been rebranded the "The 1 dad show" as I sat there among 44 mums – I counted them. I'd seen the content before, when Helen and I had attended the same event for Millie three years previously. Made to watch a video of a cartoon man chasing a woman around a bed with a pink feather, Helen and I had exchanged mirth-filled glances, trying hard not to giggle. Even then I was one of only two dads present.

This time, knowing how much I stood out and that I had to leave early, I didn't want to look like I was running away. So with 10 minutes left, I stood up, and said:

Me: *Sorry, I have to leave. I need to go and relieve the nanny.*

The laughter echoed on as I exited. My unintended one liner may even have seeded the subsequent moronic comments from Dick.

But I AM coping. Helped by a very long tail of family, friends, the meaningful support of both schools and, not least, the structures that Helen had already put in place. The challenge will come when new ones are needed as the children's world evolves.

For the next six months, or at least until Annie goes, things are actually OK if far from solid. Mentally, I feel robust, my silent mourning having begun long before Helen's death. If only I could cry though.

11.

SANCTUARY 'N' SEAGULLS

I surface from deep sleep to birdsong outside the window. It's that warm-bedded rise into consciousness that in other circumstances might invoke allusions to Ovid and his deity dream-maker Morpheus. But this is Yorkshire, not Kalamata, so better to say I'm on holiday being woken up by squawking seagulls.

It's a scene that has played out here for me for over 40 years, across generations of gulls and layers of bright paint on the pretty fishermen's cottages. Change here is rare, even as the world turns elsewhere.

Back in the 1960s my parents had the foresight to spend £1100 on a tiny cottage on the north-east coast, the location overwhelming any thought of the practicalities of its lack of kitchen or inside toilet. Fifty miles from the industrial town of my birth, it was an easy jaunt for weekends and the seeming endless hot summers of youth as remembered from rainy middle-age.

Six weeks at a time my brothers and I would roam the village and the coast around it without fear or any sense on my part that there was anything vaguely unusual in our family unit of a single adult and three children.

Looking back, coming here must have meant respite and emotional recharge for my mum. She was totally committed to her three boys and never remarried or dated until we were adults.

Our village seemed somehow to be in this world but not of it, with global events only rarely cutting through its gentle pace. Those that did still benchmark my childhood.

So it's August 1977. It's late and I'm in my bunk bed listening to Radio Luxembourg, eating midget gems, reading a comic. A perfect pre-teen evening.

Suddenly DJ Tony Prince announces:

TP: *The King is dead!*

In shock, I think: surely he means the Queen, before he goes on to say that as a mark of respect to Elvis Presley the station will cancel all its advertising that evening. Somehow that made it seem all the more significant.

I look back on the fact that I thought that at 42 Elvis had enjoyed a good innings, much the same way Pete Townshend of The Who was happy to write "Hope I die before I grow old" aged 20 and is possibly not hoping so much nowadays. Helen died older than Elvis but not by very much.

Later, in the early 1980s, I'm buying my first car from a local garage and not long afterwards am driving girl-friends to the village to see whether any of the magic of the place rubs off on them.

Visiting friends would discover that the written world

of vet James Herriot wasn't fiction after all – though one Home Counties princess was surprised to find there *were* in fact inside toilets in the north (we'd had one put in by then).

When we were both career building, I brought Helen here infrequently but with Millie and Matt's arrival we visited more often and their love of the place started to mirror my own. They entered the same fancy dress competitions in the summer fete as I had years before, but they won! They played outside for hours and went crabbing and learned to love the Magpie café in Whitby as a simple ritual pleasure on every trip.

We spent Christmases here with extended family, renting ever-posher piles as we outgrew the tiny family cottage, now owned by my brother Richard.

So when the tidal wave of Helen's death swirled through our lives it was natural to find ourselves in this place of sanctuary soon afterwards. Here, roaring seas erode the Jurassic coastline in a clumsy parallel of how Helen's death ripped at the bedrock of the happy family life that Millie, Matt and I enjoyed with her. But the cliffs still stand despite the water's fury, echoing the shape of their past while wearing a fresh face to the world. They endure. So shall we, assuming I don't screw up.

To which point I'm about to make red lights flash in the school of early bereavement best practice. I'm buying a house in the village on a whim, a wing and a prayer. Walking along the cobbled high street, I see a for sale sign on a property being sold with every knife, fork, spoon, bed and sheet in the price. Converted many years ago, run first as a tearoom and most recently as a holiday let, it has plenty of space and needs little doing before we could start using it.

I have a small amount of life assurance cash which I'd thought to use to knock down the mortgage at home, but what the hell – better to create deeper roots for Millie and Matt, a refuge where they can always come to find peace and happiness whatever else goes on in their lives. Indeed they may even be coming to visit their dad if I'm living here as a faux salty old sea-dog. A real-life version perhaps of Bernard Cribbins in *Old Jack's Boat*, a children's programme that is filmed in the village.

I take the kids for a look inside and such is their enthusiasm for it, even to the point of arguing about bedrooms, that I make the offer that day. It is accepted pretty much immediately, reflecting that the price has already come down during the year-plus it has been on the market.

It's a great feeling. I'm exultant for the first time in so long. I know Helen would approve of the decision. And, looking back, I can see how much I have changed – my natural sense of caution having been thrown to the winds by my close-up of the lesson not to offset anything to a future which may never happen.

I have one nagging doubt, though, which I put to my friend Pete's very particular brand of counsel.

Me: *Is it morally OK to have a holiday home?*
Pete: *You twat.*
Me: *Is that an answer?*

Pete: *OK, herewith the long hand. Is it going to be rented out?*

Me: *Er… yes.*

Pete: *Have you been coming here all your life supporting the local economy?*

Me: *Sort of.*

Pete: *And has fate kicked your family very hard in the nuts lately?*

Me: *Yes.*

Pete: *So only a right twat would see a problem in opening a business in a place they love, are committed to and will keep investing in for decades to come. For God's sake take off your* Guardian-reading *hair shirt and cease gazing up your own backside.*

Pete is more prophetic than he might have guessed.

Immediate family, not least Helen's parents Barbara and Ray, seem supportive of the decision even if slightly bemused by it. They're even more bemused when, in the next step towards living rather than just planning the dream, I put our Lexus saloon up for sale and look for a seven-seat estate with a roof box the size of a potting shed. But I am confident this, too, will come right. It is my intention to be able to drive to Yorkshire in a huge car packed with friends where sheer bustle and chaos disguise the fact that Helen isn't occupying any of its seven seats.

I see this house as the first tentative step towards a "new life". And who knows? One day in the distant future I might even bring a new love interest here. This is not as disloyal as it sounds even to me; the possibility was encouraged by Helen in our early conversations about my future with the kids, at a time when her death seemed a far-off, dark horizon, even with cancer confirmed. I nodded at the time in numbness rather than acceptance.

An unexpected call from James, my solicitor, dents the daydream.

Me: *I assume the searches will be fine so are we OK to complete and exchange on the same day in the summer – just in time for our holiday?*

James: *Should be OK but you need to know and accept the principle of a clause on the house's use.*

Me: *What do you mean? Can't I rent it out?*

James: *Nothing that limiting, but there's an old ecclesiastical covenant.*

Me: *You mean a chancel tax sort of thing – surely I can just insure against it?*

James: *No, it's more specific, more behavioural than that. You shouldn't promote – that may also mean practise – drunkenness or promiscuity in the vicinity.*

I'm speechless as the future fun 'n' frolic bubble bursts, leaving only my more worthy intentions. So instead I'll borrow words from one Mr Edmund Blackadder: "Fortune vomits on my eiderdown once more."

12.

GUESS WHO'S NOT
COMING TO DINNER?

I know it shouldn't matter. That it doesn't really matter. That compared to everything else that has happened and all that Helen endured and lost it is but nothing. However, has anyone seen my social life?

It's gone and almost forgotten. It was large and last seen a few weeks before Helen died. I now see that we socialised a lot right up until the end. Helen loved her friends so much and worked hard to see them even as her health failed. Now her socialising is over as finally and appallingly as anything can be. For me too, though, I realise it may never recover, as beyond former school friends, ex-colleagues and work dos, so much of it had been orchestrated by my more naturally gregarious and lovely wife.

In many ways I was always socially ambivalent, hating the thought of going out to an event with people I didn't know or would never see again; I'd be happier instead tinkering with something oily, playing at home with the kids or if leaving the house, going for a run. I'd even face the idea of an evening with friends at dinner or a party with some degree of reluctance that only the natural introvert would truly understand. I'm not *anti*-social, you understand: once I've got my foot in the door, my alter ego somehow ascends, and I can soon find myself happily working the room, often dancing in my appalling flailing-handed 1980s way without a care in the world.

Since Helen's death my aversion to stepping out into the unknown or the uncomfortable has been reinforced by my wanting to stay close to Millie and Matt, and generally having a sharpened sense of life's brevity so not being as willing to invest precious time in places and people I am not comfortable with.

Not that this last point has been tested too often of late as invitations have been most visible by their absence and my own desire to organise something has left the building, seemingly for good.

But that may now change with a dinner invitation from my close friends Luca and Charlotte. I wonder whether I'm up to it. Will there be a trigger point as we sit down to dinner in their home, which sees me dissolve in my own tears as I finally find a way to cry like the mythical squonk? It would certainly be a downer on the other guests' evening.

I discuss the invitation with a close confidante at work. Patience – despite never being widowed, indeed never having married and seemingly happiest on horseback – has a powerful instinct for human nature and social intercourse. She is also very kind and while not much older than me makes me feel like the passing years have bestowed her with wisdom instead of the grey hairs and love handles gifted by my own advancing timeline. As I share my very real fear of falling apart in public with her, she considers a moment before replying in a well-spoken but authoritative voice as if telling a reluctant pony to get back down the pit.

Patience: *Look, Adam, you'll be fine. Maybe try and find out who the other guests are. Ideally, you'd barely know them, which will make it easier to avoid going places in the conversation that you'll find hard. They won't feel they have to acknowledge or even talk about Helen if they didn't know her!*

It's longhand logic but good advice and I discover that indeed I barely know the other guests, which may suggest that Luca and Charlotte are in league with Patience or at least have the same good instincts.

Even so the day before the dinner, I'm jittery and find myself moaning to Millie:

Me: *Are you sure you'll be OK if I go out tomorrow? It's no issue for me to cancel – Luca and Charlotte will understand.*

She spots immediately that I'm trying to back out of it. Unimpressed and with an expression that makes it no doubt whose daughter she is (somewhere between compassion and exasperation with the latter winning), she lets fly:

Millie: *Daaaaaaad – go! You've spent weeks with Matt and me here, taking us out and about to music, karate, ballet and everything else – Mum wouldn't want you to never go out yourself.*

She grins, knowing that it's a knockout blow and I've lost – but she is right. Of course the kids don't want their dad to be a hermit.

Matt walks past, once more demonstrating that he has acute hearing and a mind that is always looking for the deal:

Matt: *Yeah, Dad, go out. It's what Mum would want. I'm just thinking, though, if you're enjoying yourself can we have a pizza delivered so we do too?*

Not for the first time it's apparent that I am living a smaller-scale, sadder version of the TV comedy show *Outnumbered*. I smile wryly to myself as both kids have done to me what I have so far avoided doing to them – invoking their late mum's memory to get across a point they want to win. I avoid doing this only to keep my powder dry for things that really might matter, such as:

Me: *You mum would have wanted you to go to University.*

Or even…

Me: *Your mum wouldn't want you to walk home at 4am from the party… etc etc.*

I'm also very mindful of the *Only Fools and Horses* warning against devaluing a mother's love by invoking it too often to get one's way:

Rodney: *Whatever the subject is, Mum had something to say about it on her death bed. She must have spent her final few hours in this mortal realm doing nothing but rabbiting!*

Neither Helen nor I had really understood until late on that she was on her own death bed and our last, gentle, honest conversations remain unpublished. For the record they had nothing to do with dinner parties.

So I go to the dinner and... have a great evening.

Patience was spot on. Barely knowing the other guests makes it easier as our not talking about Helen or my bereavement feels natural, not forced. I suspect some quiet briefing by Charlotte has helped and my mind's eye pictures her interviewing prospective dinner guests for suitability earlier in the day, rejecting any subject to histrionics or morbid curiosity. Thank you, Charlotte.

The only wobble comes when I walk through into the dining room and see that there are only five places set for dinner – my first odd-number event. But hey, life is going to be full of these unexpected emotional ambushes so, in a piece of poor DIY life coaching, I tell myself to "frigging get on with it".

And before I know it, more gently and significantly than I could have imagined, kind people, fab food and outstanding home-mixed limoncello nudge me back into the social saddle. Patience would approve even if I'm still far from a gallop.

13.

Pussycat, Pussycat, I Love You

I'm staring lovingly across the table into beautiful, unblinking deep blue eyes.

Their owner is returning my gaze with a frosty disdain before peering balefully back down at the fish dish I've placed before them. There's momentary calm, then he jumps up and without breaking stride runs out of the kitchen into the garden straight to the top of a huge maple tree, startling the starlings.

So exits Harry, our beautiful Siberian Forest cat, whose presence is such a joy to Millie, Matt and me. He was Helen's pet, bought after a lifetime of loving cats but never being able to have one due to being very allergic to them.

After her diagnosis, lifetime aspirations were suddenly more pressing. Sandwiched between chemotherapy, radiotherapy, invasive treatments, grim-faced or overly cheery consultants, her job and the beautiful normality of a busy household, she'd found time for a catty fact-find and posed a question that could only ever have ended one way – love and illness do that.

Helen: *I really want a cat. I really do. How about it?*

Our first thought was to try and source a specially bred hypoallergenic kitten. But that plan was soon scuppered, not so much by the £2000 price tag – I would have sacrificed anything to find the money – but by the two-year waiting list. To those with cancer and their loved ones time is no longer just an acquaintance but a stalking adversary.

As ever, though, I'd underestimated Helen's rigour and vigour, as with the same easy smile that accompanied her whole love of life, she announced:

Helen: *Fortunately, I have an alternative. The Siberian Forest cat is not only the national cat of Russia but apparently has less of the Fel D1 protein that I react to in its saliva. And there's a breeder with a litter just up the road!*

Me: *Whehay!*

Helen (laughing): *It's still £600 and there was a waiting list.*

Me: *Oh! But how do you mean "was"?*

Helen: *They were all taken but apparently someone has dropped out and the youngest is available. We can go on Saturday for me to have a roll around.*

It was actually 80 miles "up the road" but this was no issue as Helen was so animated that her excitement was fabulously infectious as the four of us headed off. We met the mother cat in a breeder's house full of chaos and kittens. Helen rolled around with six of them, then Millie and Matt, and finally after some encouragement, so too did I.

There among the pile of paws and fluffy ears was the youngest – "ours", if Helen didn't react. Far from being the runt of the litter he was the largest. White with blue eyes and a faint red marking on his tail, he was not just a Siberian but a Neva Masquerade, a breed found near the river Neva in Russia. As he grew, his red point markings would increase on his face so he'd look as if he were wearing a mask.

After an hour we left, agreeing to let the breeder know that evening. I was by this time feeling apprehensive as I'd spotted that although she wasn't wheezing, one of Helen's eyes had swollen up. En route home we stopped for a tea and had a quiet chat out of the children's extremely long earshot.

Me: *You're reacting. Your eye…*
Helen: *…is fine.*
Me: *It really is reacting you know.*
Helen: *There's probably something in it. It's fine. If that's the only reaction after an hour with seven cats all over me in a hairy house, one small kitten is not going to be a problem.*

She looked at me meaningfully, not inviting nor receiving further dissent.

Helen: *I hope he won't be one of those snooty cats or spend his life hiding from people. I want him to be happy to sit on my desk purring when I'm working... what's wrong?*

She was so excited. So happy that waiting a few weeks and paying a small king's ransom was neither here nor there. My expression showed a wave of upset that Helen was talking about their future together when such a future was so unknown. Her green eyes met mine in an understanding of silent mutual pain – it was another of those moments of oneness in which illness had undcrlined our love of each other and our lives together.

So a few weeks later Harry came home – named by Millie and Matt after the "boy who lived", a link to a sweet recent past when their mother would read aloud the Harry Potter books. These stories filled their childhoods and still provide comfort at night, as they listen to CDs narrated by the brilliant Stephen Fry.

For the first two days our Harry hid under the sofa but then gloriously came and stayed out. Better still, when Helen was stroking him, he'd purr deeply like an outboard motor at full throttle in sharp contrast to his high-pitched mewing.

His paws were huge, rears longer than fronts. Was this usual? Returning to the website Helen had used, I read up to the point about the protein and unlike Helen kept reading beyond the bottom of the page.

The different paw lengths were, it seems, normal but were part of a comprehensive description that included the fact that "The Siberian forest cat is the second largest domestic cat breed and over five years can grow to 25lb!"

We bought a bigger cat flap.

Harry's size provides a big barrel-chested presence but he's very gentle. He's still mainly white but as reported to Ruth has been yellow (poisonous lily pollen), brown (poisonous creosote) and orange (rusty tank in loft) and each time scrubbed in the bath without much complaint. Indeed, he runs his head under the tap for fun, comes when you call, sits when asked and will hunt you out to lie beside you anywhere in the house. In short Harry is and was everything that Helen hoped for.

She saw something almost spiritual in him and in many ways he was a more accessible, more credible source of comfort to her than the decision she took a few months before her death to be baptised. Sorry, vicar, but there it is.

Today he is still Helen's adored friend and in Harry we remember her joy in a living, furry form. Somehow he anchors us back to being a family of four and is a tree-climbing, picky-eating symbol of our love for Helen. Cat is too short a word for so humungous a comfort.

14.

MEMORIAL MARATHON

The landline rings and I grit my teeth. For so long a link to loved ones, with the rise of the mobile it has instead become the weapon of choice for scammers and "How are you today?" cold-callers.

"Hello, it's Carrie," says a too-friendly female voice.

I do a quick mental Rolodex through the Carries I know, drawing a blank but feeling an inexplicably negative association to the name as if it were a school teacher who had been mean to me or a cocktail that I'd over-indulged on long ago.

Assuming it's a cold call, my voice hardens:

Me: *So what do you want, Carrie?*

Carrie (unctuous tone surviving the coldness in my voice): *I was wondering if you have decided what to do with Helen?*

Physics dictates you never hear the bullet that hits you, but I hear this one just as it tears the breath from me in the shock of hearing my wife referred to in the present tense. It's the first time this has happened and Carrie's words pile into sensibilities already pummelled by bereavement.

Me (stammering): *I'm sorry but Helen has died. My wife died. My wife Helen has died.*

A moment's pause.

Carrie: *It's Carrie, we met when you made the arrangements for Helen. I wondered if you had decided what you wanted to do with her ashes.*
Me: *Sorry.*
Carrie: *The funeral directors?*
Me: *Could you give me a moment, please?*
Carrie (cheerily): *Of course. As long as you like.*

The conversion of present tense to ashes hits me like a blow to my solar plexus. I slowly fold onto the stairs by the phone. This Carrie is the woman I'd sat opposite arranging Helen's funeral in her all-too-quick transformation from loved wife, mother, daughter and sister to "her body".

To be fair it's not really Carrie's fault I feel this way even if her demeanour could have been a bit less like I was due to pick up the dry cleaning and had forgotten about it.

Her words dragged me back a few weeks to the hospital half an hour after Helen had died and the night sister had approached me, asking in heavily accented mainland European English:

Night Sister: *Have you made any arrangements for the body?*
Me: *What?*
Night Sister: *The body. Have you made arrangements for it to be removed? Our regulations require the body to be removed within six hours of death.*

My reaction makes me blush now but at least I remained relatively quiet, hissing the words out of respect for ill patients in other rooms:

Me: *What the hell are you talking about? I'll assume that you're referring to my wife and partner of 26 years within minutes of her dying as "the body" is some sort of problem you have with the English language. The alternative being that you are the most insensitive bitch ever to put on a nurse's uniform. Funnily enough I don't have a funeral director lined up waiting nor should you mistake me for someone who gives a toss what your self-made bloody regulations are. If there's a problem get someone on the phone or out of his or her fucking bed and down here now. Did you understand that then, sister? Either way piss off and leave me with my wife.*

Gordon Ramsey might be OK with that sort of outburst but I'm not. To be fair it seemed to work – she did leave me alone at that point to make arrangements, no more mention being made of Helen aka "the Body".

Since that dreadful night I'm more used to my widower status and don't need to let off steam to be able to function in the face of crass adversity, I think. So now I choose calmness, not confrontation. I return to the Carrie call:

Me: *You mean her... collecting them? Her ashes...*
Carrie: *Yes.*
Me: *Please may I call you back when I've decided?*

I put the phone down immediately. I assume their £5000 bill included indefinite storage of a small urn.

Carrie's question should not have been a surprise but I have buried its coming because of the shocking gap between Helen, the vital, ever-optimistic force of nature who was so full of life, and her new status as an urn full of ashes.

Carrie's quest, no doubt for reasons of storage logistics, evokes a knottier problem as to where ultimately they will be laid to rest – even that language sucks. In fact the whole business is one that I hate, I never want to lay eyes on any urn and would happily leave it there for the foreseeable future.

What to do with a loved one's ashes is yet another bastard question that I never in my life saw being asked so I turn immediately to the ever-friendly folk at WAY. There, I find every version of my angst and a cornucopia of confirmation and inspiration. From sprinkling ashes at home, at sea, on a favourite walk, in a garden of remembrance to being mounted on the mantelpiece, shot skywards in a firework or even fashioned into jewellery.

Every option is clearly the right one for those concerned and perhaps wrong for me.

WAY's input is also a reminder that I am not the only stakeholder in this decision. Helen's parents, Barbara and Ray, her sister, Sarah, and the kids need to feel "rightness" in what we do.

Lying awake into the early hours, I know for a fact that for me, the urn and its dark contents are not my wife.

Helen lives in the vibrancy, laughter and love of Millie and Matt. She lives in the values she bequeathed them; not as something inert and spent. She lives in every happy memory and at the happy heart of the life I may yet go on to live. I don't need or want her ashes in any way; I particularly don't want to see them in a plastic urn, hold it or have it anywhere close to hand.

There was a moment, a few minutes after Helen died, when I sensed a shift. Holding her hands, some 10 minutes after she had breathed out for the last time, something passed from her, something not identifiable and of which I was not even aware until it had gone. I struggle with religion generally and do not have the language to be able to say for certain that what I sensed was her soul or spirit passing peacefully on. I do know, however, that it absolutely happened.

This certainty made even more macabre the wild panic I felt some two hours later when, fitfully dozing on a camp bed, I sprang fully alert at what sounded like breathing – someone gasping for breath. It was coming from where Helen lay on the hospital mattress, on which some sort of air-driven technology to prevent bed sores had been left powered up and had chosen that moment to vent. It took me a while to calm down because of the shock rather than any sense Helen might still be with me, so dissociated was the figure on the bed from the women I loved.

If Helen's lifeless form meant little to me other than being a reminder of her loss, her ashes would mean even less, but I understood well enough that I was creating a memorial for the living rather than a last resting place for the dead. Wherever Helen is it is not in that urn.

The obvious thing was to investigate a memorial in the form of a more traditional grave, one that anyone could visit on his or her terms. I had hoped this might be in the pretty town-centre churchyard where Helen's funeral service was held but had discovered to my surprise that this was out of the question:

Vicar: *The churchyard is closed, I'm afraid, to new burials.*

Me: *Churchyards close?*

Vicar: *They do when full and that one I'm afraid has been closed for some years.*

Me: *They are only ashes rather than a whole body – surely that is OK?*

Vicar: *Not if you wanted a full-size memorial. You could place her ashes in the garden of remembrance.*

Me: *What does that mean? Do the ashes get randomly scattered?*

Vicar: *No, they are placed behind a stone within the wall there or in the ground – the children could visit it anytime they were in town.*

Me (thinking): *Nooooooo.*

The closure was a kick up the pants at the time but I realise now it was a blessing in disguise. The last thing Millie and Matt needed was to have to walk past the site where their mother was buried every time they went out – to a friend's house, party or just for a milk shake. It would make them feel no doubt the same as walking past the funeral director's does for me today, knowing Helen's ashes are in there – eye-wateringly, red-wine-quaffingly, stay-up-too-lately dreadful.

It didn't help when I took a look at the garden of remembrance accompanied by a lady vicar. It looked a little shabby.

Me: *It's certainly peaceful but I'm not sure it's right?*
Vicar: *Of course it has to work for you. Any reason in particular?*
Me: *I think the whole location, being in town, is too central to the kids' lives. Also, to be honest, it looks like the sort of place I'd come to drink cider with friends if I was 15 and living here.*

She didn't reply although we both stole a glance at an empty can of Strongbow nestling under the stone bench.

So the hunt went on and a few weeks later I'm standing beside the council's cemetery officer, Claire, who is kind and helpful in a way that suggests it is because of who she is, not just how she has been trained.

On paper this place doesn't seem too promising either,

being near a school and busy railway line. On the day, though, these are massive positives as the glorious mature trees and bushes of the immaculate cemetery are flanked by vibrant life in the running of the trains and the shouts and cries of happy primary-age kids.

Less good was standing next to Claire gazing at the next plot due for sale. It was horrific – a row of recent graves with plain crosses awaiting monuments. Each had a pile of recently dug earth laid out in the unmistakable shape of the coffin underneath whose space it had once filled.

Too much for the kids. Too much for me now.

Walking into the older section, I see a plot closer to what I had in mind – end of a row, under a tree and by a bench surrounded by mature graves. I'm not hopeful but ask Claire:

Me: *Could I buy this one, please?*
Claire: *It would be unusual. We normally wouldn't be able to sell a plot so close to the tree because of the roots.*
Me: *But we're not burying a body…*
Claire: *I know, which is why, maybe, we can sell it to you.*

I see again how kind people can be, even within the awfulness of every facet of having this conversation. One gets used to knockbacks so when they don't come it really is moving.

Things don't progress, however. I sign but don't post payment for the plot and don't call Carrie back. A sort of sadness madness descends between me and the whole subject of interring Helen's remains.

The eclectic list of my varied hobbies and passions – aircraft, classic cars, film, motorbikes, marathons, Formula 1, karate, my hero Sammy Davis Jr., the saxophone, Donna Leon and general DIY – now includes gravestones. I'm looking around zealously, perhaps feverishly for inspiration for a memorial for Helen's beautiful plot, overlooking the fact that I haven't actually bought it.

This exercise finds me unable to drive past a cemetery without taking a look. On occasion in the rain I have driven into a few designed for Victorian carriages, not huge Volvos, and so become horribly wedged.

I sense that this quest for inspiration has become the goal and I am drawing out the exercise to fill a void. It has become a distraction and cause of too much late-night angst and excess booze. Note to self – if you find yourself drinking something blue you bought at Duty Free in Norway in 2004 it is time to give your behaviour a long, hard stare. I need help.

I share my angst with my friend and pub provocateur Pete who comes straight out with an answer which suggests he is saying something he has been thinking for a while but now has permission to say:

Pete: *You are driven to do nothing because nothing is better than losing control. Grief created a control freak even before Helen died and this is just the latest example of it.*

I asked for it but I'm confused at this and not a little pissed off, and look it. He laughs, before nailing me with my own borrowed homily:

Pete: *OK, soft lad. You say the hard part of a marathon is not the last mile but the first step.*

Me (drily): *Yes, I have been known to say that.*

Pete: *Just a bit! You're avoiding taking the first solid step of burying Helen because you're afraid of how you'll feel when this quest is over and you no longer have anything "to do" for her – so she slips a little further away. That's tough after being her primary supporter but may I say by doing sod all you've lost control anyway.*

Me: *Not fair. It's because I can't bear to think about it – the ashes…*

Pete: *I get that but dare I suggest she needs you to get over this and do this last thing, not just for her but also for her family whom you are probably worried about alienating if you don't get it right.*

Me: *Getting it right means…?*

Pete: *How do I know? It definitely means you letting go and involving them. What I also know is that getting it wrong involves doing nothing. Get on with it – you'll know as you go if it's right and everyone will feel closer, not further away – and that includes Helen.*

It is hard to admit even to myself but he has struck a chord. I feel ashamed. When Helen was ill I overcame my fear of needles, putting in lines and using syringes to save her extra hospital trips. But now with my indecision and general failure to progress on anything to do with her burial I am failing Helen in this last chance to care for her mortal self.

Me (exhaling long and loudly): *OK. Another pint?*

Pete: *See what I mean. You're uncertain how to react to being told off and are trying to seize control with beer!*

Me: *What?*

Pete: *It's my round but you are taking the initiative to offer me another and so control the moment. I'll have a Guinness, though. It's thirsty work being right all the time!*

This is the toughest love anyone has passed my way in months – probably since Helen herself – but Pete has gentle wisdom wrapped in hammer-to-the-head helpfulness.

He's noticed, probably ages ago, something bigger than the issue of Helen's burial, something I thought hidden. In recent years the trajectory of our lives careered out of control due to the brutal stewardship of Helen's fucking cancer but this forced me to try and at least control the logistics of illness and treatment. Since her death this has extended to desperately trying to reassert direction to the rudderless wreck of everything that Millie, Matt and I had thought of as normality. The unintended consequences of which now threaten to leave Helen's ashes abandoned. No longer.

I post the payment for the cemetery plot. And, at her father Ray's inspired suggestion, we commission a simple but very distinctive slate monument, carved beautifully with a copy of a picture we have of *The Owl and the Pussy-Cat* which meant so much to Helen, as well as the first two lines from Carol Ann Duffy's "Words, Wide Night" which she had chosen for her memorial service and which I use in the opening of this book.

At last, with the support of Helen's family, I have taken the first and second steps towards laying her to rest.

These make the other 26.218 metaphorical marathon miles look a lot less daunting.

15.

BRAS, BALLET & BRAVADO

1:am finds me sitting on the sofa, slightly drunk, near naked and in pain. I'm staring in disbelief at a needle plunged deep into my inner thigh. I take a deep breath and pull it out, collapsing back exhausted but not finished.

I have tried so hard over recent weeks for my safety and sanity not to be up at this time, stressed and on the outside of too much alcohol – particularly spirits.

Tonight I've failed big time but this isn't a version of *Trainspotting*, chronicling a bereaved husband's descent from mainstream coping to middle-class mainlining. It's another example of how hard I'm paddling to keep our new normality afloat amid the choppy stream of logistical and lifestyle challenges that Helen would have handled seamlessly had she lived.

Today had gone so well at first with the simple, innocent pleasure of shopping for Millie's ballet pointe shoes. It was to be her first class the following day and she was very excited at having landed a rare place on the popular programme. For weeks she had been seeking to strengthen her calves using dynamic tension with what looked like giant elastic bands. The whole thing for someone like me, whose school had rugby four days a week with an option for more, was a fascinating alien planet but one filled with pride and wonder.

We'd travelled together into Covent Garden (where else) to a shop that was clearly the inner sanctum of all things ballet. Sandy, the helpful assistant who looked little older than Millie, led us through a ballerinafest of satin and silk footwear.

Inevitably, the winners were very pricey and very pink.

Sandy: *These are just a little bit more but are the ones I'd choose, particularly if you are new to pointe.*
Me: *Millie?*
Millie: *They are the best fit for sure so yes, please, Dad!*

Distracted by the bill, Millie's passion and the poignancy of an exciting new experience for her that Helen wasn't part of, I didn't really take enough notice of the next bit:

Sandy: *Here are the ribbons. Of course, you'll need to measure them and of course if you have problems there are great videos on YouTube.*

Fast-forward to midnight after a lovely dad 'n' daughter dinner in Wagamama. I hold open the shoebox and four matching pale pink ribbons flutter onto the sofa, patently unattached to the pricey shoes.

It seems that the conversation with Sandy should have gone:

Sandy: *You'll need to measure the ribbons before sewing them into the shoes.*

Me: *What do you mean sew the ribbons?*

Sandy: *The ribbons are to hold the shoes on but need to be cut to the right length for the dancer's legs.*

Me: *Oh God how hard is that?*

Sandy: *Don't worry, there are YouTube videos to help if you get stuck. Be careful when you singe the ends.*

Me: *Millie, let's get home quickly if you need these tomorrow!*

Of course I'll gloss over the question why for circa £60 a pair one end couldn't be sewn in place already and the other simply cut to suit.

Anyway that wasn't what happened and it had been midnight when the clock struck 12 and my fairytale evening ended. This is a shame as I could do with being the Brothers Grimm's old shoemaker who slept soundly, knowing that elves would finish the shoes during the night.

Instead, I'm sewing, swearing and drinking in equal measures. Twice I stagger upstairs to wake a sleeping Millie to check her leg length before I cut the ribbons. In practice, if not intent, it is a bad dad masterclass.

I watch the YouTube videos whose calm confidence and eager-beaver instruction contrast sharply with my boxer-clad, amateur-hour attempts not to ruin her shoes.

Despite losing, and painfully finding, the needle

a couple of times, I finish sewing before 2am and actually I'm quite pleased – it's a neat job, a throwback perhaps to my mother's not inconsiderable professional accomplishments in the fashion world.

The final challenge is to singe the ends of the ribbons on the gas ring to stop them fraying. To be fair, the videos don't mention using the cooker for this task, and as I watch the flames run up the end like a pink fuse I realise a match or lighter really would have been better. I put it out with minimum damage but maximum pulse rate as I blow frantically at the flames.

So the shoes are finished and all is well. Next day Millie goes to her class beaming. That night I get a message from Jennie, her pointe teacher, complimenting me on the quality of the sewing in the shoes. She has three daughters and knows our back-story and I'm sure she's being kind, but with sore fingers, a dull throb behind the eyes and a plaster on my thigh I'll take the compliments wherever and whenever they come my way. In the battle to rebuild, any victory is sweet, although many are bittersweet.

The fact is that I might have ended up sewing on the ribbons even if Helen were alive because I'm better at it. The massive and to me heartbreaking difference is that Helen would have spotted the need to attach them by listening to Sandy – and here's the thing, would have bought the shoes weeks ago.

We were great together and gone with her is one half of a not perfect but pretty bleeding complementary team.

It is not just about new skills. Helen's absence requires new knowledge. Sitting at the laptop, Millie and I are buying bras. This is definitely one that Helen would have handled but Millie seems happy to shop with me and while not on trial I feel the need to be both competent and cool.

Also and not least I want to get it right because so far Millie has done much of this herself, guessing badly her size before ordering online. Consequently I've taken enough bras back to shops on a Saturday morning that the assistants are beginning to recognise, possibly not in a good way, the middle-aged bloke with a penchant for seemingly randomly chosen 32B/32C/34B/34C teen foundation garments.

Tonight Millie's enthusiastic face is front-lit by a screen displaying what looks to me like lingerie rather than utilitarian underwear. She provides commentary:

Millie: *Dad, this one's designed to provide maximum support.*
Me: *It looks a bit racy to me!*
Millie: *That's probably because it's a sports bra, Dad.*

I peer suspiciously, pretty sure that the three "P's" in the description, *push-up, plunge* and *padded* are not the language of fitness but of display.

However, I've learned to save my sanity by choosing battles carefully, so hit "checkout" without hesitation. She grins – she has roped in her mark and worked the sting.

The challenge is not just that I'm a male having to deal with a teenage girl. Matt's need for help with his homework, mediation of fallouts with friends, music exams and much more, all need input that would probably have been better from Helen.

I'm not complaining too hard, it is what it is, but I keep getting caught out not just by the obviously greater work-load of one rather than two parents, but also by the loss of these joint skills and experiences. I'm coping but only just, often relying on logistical firefighting skills for fires I have lit due to lack of timely understanding or action.

More damaging is that the sheer overload makes me at times far more snappy, unfair and unkind to the kids and I hate myself for this.

Add to this the fact that I am working full on in a demanding job and the stress is beginning to show. I'm not sleeping enough, not eating enough and drinking too much. The weight loss I sought in order to get fitter is uncontrolled and I'm starting to look gaunt rather than thin.

I have to get better at dealing with day-to-day demands, many of which I can't even guess at, but which I do know are likely to get tougher as the children get older. Cliché though it is, I struggle most when these needs are concurrent and multi-layered in demanding the empathy and action which Helen achieved so well and so often. The children need their mother and don't have her any more. How sad does that sound? How close can any man get to providing a substitute for that nurturing close connection begun in the womb. Can I? Even before Helen died I would have put a figure on my personality in terms of gender bias of 70/30 maybe – that's 70% northern blokey bloke, 30% man who makes an effort at being sensitive and emotionally expressive, particularly around the kids. Now though, for the challenges of coming months and years, 70/30 maybe needs to reverse to 30/70 for a while if we are going to thrive, not just survive. Even in my eyes, wishing to change one's gender bias in this way is a tragicomic ambition and one that doesn't need casual commentators or comedians, so mum is the word in every way.

Until I get there I simply need more time so that everything is not last minute. Of the things to jettison the one I am least in love with is the job which has lost its gloss because it takes me away from home too often.

Somehow I feel I am on borrowed time, which is ironic given how long I spent with someone who truly was. Not ironic, in fact, but shameful when I have a choice and a chance to change things in a way Helen didn't.

Change is a-coming.

16.

WHO WANTS TO LIVE FOREVER? ME!

It's not a happy thought but my family's middle-aged males are stalked by the grim reaper, whose icy fingers reach out for the smokers, the unfit, the overweight and the complacent.

Death took my father in his late 50s, my half-brother in his 60s, and narrowly missed my brother and cousin in their mid-50s.

This male issue seems to be on my father's side as female family members, with the appalling exception now of Helen, and men on my mother's side sail on to a great age in rude heath. Hence, when elderly relatives say, "You look like your dad," they mean well, but I hear only the horror of "You're marked for early death, sonny!"

It is one of the reasons why I love it that Millie takes more after me and Matt his mother, so providing some protection from my homespun but alarming theory.

With Helen's death, my unease at this perceived frailty has turned to panic, not because of any intrinsic fear of dying but because Millie and Matt need their surviving parent to stick around, and even though I am not ill in any way separation anxiety is occurring more and more often since Helen's funeral.

The other day, leaving the kids in the car, I ran into the shop to buy cat food for the ever-hungry Harry. With an unscheduled chat to a passing school mum, I'm not back for 20 minutes rather than the forecast 10. Millie and Matt are anxious to the point of tears:

Matt: *Where were you, Dad?*
Millie: *We thought something bad had happened to you.*

The kids need me now, tomorrow and years from now – definitely past the mid-50s danger zone. So I in my turn need to love life and myself as never before.

The trouble is that male chromosomes in general seem to carry a doctor-dodging gene, such that blokes have to be at death's door before even consulting a GP. Also, as a crude rule of thumb, the closer the problem lies to our willies or generally "down there" the less likely we blokes are to bother the doctor's receptionist. Just sayin'.

I start in a better place than most men to beat the rap of family history not only because my personality's female facets make the doc's waiting room less trial by ordeal, but also because I've never smoked, have always exercised and, after a recent return to fitness, am leaner than ever. Importantly, perhaps most importantly, after sitting with Helen in so many hospitals and doctor's waiting rooms, my fear of them has totally gone.

The sheer frailty of life is now something so clear to me. When people would say before *"without your health you have nothing"* I'd think little of it but now understand it is absolutely and totally everything. Everything. Helen's courage lights the way forward; a total lack of fuss facing so much invasive treatment and, at its worst, more needles in a day than I have faced in my entire life.

So I have embarked on a course of self-induced, largely self-funded medical tests. I have been poked, prodded and scanned, given armfuls of blood, had a heart scan for calcium build-up and endured the daddy of them all, a colonoscopy, albeit in my case one without presenting symptoms:

Consultant: *It's unusual for someone to do this electively. Are you sure you want to proceed?*

Me: *Definitely.*

Consultant: *It's true that if there's nothing worrying found now, you are likely to be fine for some years to come. It is, though, very unusual to put yourself through it.*

I suddenly wondered whether he thought I had psychological problems or perhaps simply enjoyed having things poked up my bum on a Tuesday morning. So I asked the question doctors hate:

Me: *What would you do?*

Consultant (unhesitatingly): *Do it. I had one myself for the same reason.*

I feel suddenly we are brothers in arms, or maybe in arse. As I write this I'm suppressing an image of him self-administering a Box Brownie up his own backside.

Me: *OK. Let's do it!*

So a week later, I'm lying on a trolley wearing a pair of "modesty pants"; most ill named given they have a huge slit up the back. We all know why.

Consultant: *We'll give you something to make you woozy, but you'll be awake and can watch on the screen. We'll be with you in a few minutes.*

It has been a hard week in what has been a series of many hard weeks and late nights. When next I open my eyes, the consultant is looming over me.

Consultant: *I'm not sure if it is a first, but you are the only person I've ever had who has slept through the procedure without any help from us.*

So I missed the world's most bizarre TV show – up my own colon – but it was all clear. Add this good news to clear arteries, the blood pressure of a 30-year-old, a resting heart rate under 60, and I ponder the irony that my wife's legacy to me, other than the kids and a dodgy Rolf Harris-signed painting, may be 30 years more of life with Millie and Matt than she had. I thank you,

Helen, for this as I do pretty much everything else that is good in my life.

17.

KAREN KISSES ME CONSCIOUS...

"Please place this ring on Helen's finger," asked the pink trouser-suited minister as she handed me the band of gold.

Helen and I had discussed our vows the previous evening in the back of a cab en route to our hotel, making the decision to go for the more traditional wording. This view was supported in full by the cheerfully chubby cab driver.

Driver: *My second wedding we chose something more modern but as vows go it just didn't feel right so for the third I went traditional.*

Helen and I were still giggling as we checked into our huge hotel.

Traditional felt right and would offset some of the elements which were absolutely not so. OK our rings had come from Asprey in Mayfair and the church was a proper one by local standards but given those local standards were defined by the fact we were in Las Vegas, pretty much anything went. We played Black Jack and Poker in lieu of a reception and had Tom Jones performing "It's Not Unusual" live as our first dance. Women still threw their pants at him, albeit in larger sizes than in the 60s, I'm guessing.

Our wedding was frankly pretty bleeding unusual among our peer group but it was only after we spent summers at so many formal weddings in marquees up and down the land that Helen and I had decided to cut loose and do our own thing. We'd told no one of our Nevada intentions before heading for the beautiful giant theme park that the US is for Brits and nobody suspected anything – we were not even engaged, despite having been together for eight years, co-habiting for two of them.

We'd at least chosen the more sober Little Church of the West, knowing we'd leave it with beaming smiles no smaller than Elvis's and Anne Margaret's, when it was the backdrop to their wedding scene finale in the film *Viva Las Vegas*. Helen and I were full of life and hope.

Flash forward 15 years and sitting in the intimate deadness of the Yorkshire night drinking wine and chatting with an attractive single woman, I realise for the first time that the vows made on that hot Vegas morning no longer apply. The last line of which, immersed in each other and the excitement of marriage, we never for a moment thought anything of – *"In sickness and in health until death do us part"* – the unwelcome permission to move on if bereaved which no one ever wants to be granted.

In the same way, when I told Helen, "I give you this ring as a symbol of our vows," I never imagined taking it off the finger that I'd nervously placed it on. But I did so, sliding it off her lifeless hand, tip to tip, flesh to flesh, our fingers even closer than those in Michelangelo's masterpiece *The Creation of Adam* – irony upon irony. This was only minutes after she died, the ring joining the one she placed on my hand with such joy all those happy years previously.

Looking down at them together, hers shinier having not endured the same trial by toolbox rummaging that mine had, I stood in that dreadful hospital room and declared to myself "I'll never, ever take them off" in what turned out to be dishonest death-bed bravado.

For a while, particularly over the endless period between Helen's death and her funeral, I took comfort in rolling both bands around my finger like 22-carat worry beads.

But the brutal truth is that I'm no longer married, and once I'd returned to the facade of our normal life's routines, even looking at them became a source of misery. It was like carrying in my hand a bucket of iced water ready to drench even the faintest moment of positivity. The rings, so long cherished, had become a tragic totem of loss, not love.

Then there were the "gruesome glances" when sitting with friends and colleagues. I would see them flashing subtle looks at my left hand. Not everyone but many. I could estimate their ring-cycle of unspoken concern.

Over a 30-minute cup of coffee it would play out:

> *"Oh my, he's still wearing his wedding ring."*
> *"That's lovely."*
> *"But is he in denial?"*
> *"Oh it's not a Russian wedding ring but a second one.*
> *He must be wearing Helen's too. Poor Adam."*
> *"That's lovely but a bit macabre."*
> *"I hope he is not going to cry."*
> *"He must have small fingers."*

So a few days after the funeral I decided to stop wearing them in what is still one of the hardest decisions of this whole journey. Rather than going cold turkey, I threaded them on a gold chain around my neck that I hoped no one would spot. This was worse in many ways as their unaccustomed bling made me feel more middle-aged Home Counties Puff Daddy than grieving widower and having them dangling somehow underlined even more that the warm finger of the warm hand and warm body on which Helen's had been placed was gone for good.

My newly naked fingers provide a strange sense of freedom and relief – with immediate and ensuing guilt. However, what I hadn't factored in – those people who are long bereaved will smile at this – is that while a wedding ring sends out a signal of unavailability, being without one at a certain age sends a different message – what, specifically, I don't know, but it seems to have changed my status in an unfathomable way. I never look at or notice jewellery at all but I get that others do, particularly the third finger of the left hand.

In my career I've stayed alone in many hotels in several countries. Naturally a bit shy, I have still managed to strike up cheery conversations in bars. Booze helps.

These have included with women on their own and the only weird stuff has occasionally been someone asking me to invest in a dodgy scheme or "keep in touch" despite little contact or much in common. To be fair, I have always, even in my early 20s, been dreadful at spotting signs that women might be vaguely interested in me and time has not been a great healer of my lack of a flirt alert.

So I'm sitting in the pub in the seaside village in Yorkshire where I've bought a house, tapping away on my laptop and scoffing dinner. I'm in a really upbeat mood, having come back to the UK early from a Stateside trip. I realise that no one knows where I am and that childcare is covered. So I contrive to head north and visit the place that has always provided physical refuge and emotional recharge.

It is evening and I'm working on my laptop happily eating chops and chips when suddenly a pair of liquid brown eyes and a long furry wet nose appear over the lid. The nose is twitching madly as its owner savours and slavers at the meaty scent from my plate and is soon joined by a pair of heavy brown Labrador paws on the table edge.

Dog Lady: *Honey, get down! I'm so sorry. She didn't lick anything, did she?*

I look up at the pleasant voice's owner. The woman had been sitting at the table near mine, also eating alone, albeit with a large brown dog tucked at her feet.

Me: *I like dogs. Don't worry. Nothing slobbered over. She is lovely. Aren't you, Honey?*

I stroke the friendly chocolate Lab, who likes the attention, laughing open-mouthed into my face. Honey's owner is blonde-haired, youngish, softly spoken.

Dog Lady: *Thank you. I make her lie down but she's learned how to crawl like a commando along the floor following her nose then popping up in front of whoever's dinner's most appealing. Usually it's OK but sometimes she gets her tongue in or shocks people into spilling something. I've tried tying her to the leg but she's taken a few tables with her.*

Her name is Karen, she's in her late 30s, single and renting a cottage locally to spend a few days *"getting her head together"*. She's attractive, with an effervescence that lends itself to easy conversation, and her joy in her temporary time out from her own life touches a chord with my own sense of escape.

We chat easily, demob-happy comrades. After I mention that I've been away and am looking forward to seeing the kids again, she asks me:

Dog Lady/Karen: *How often do you have them?*

Me: *Usually 24/7 365 days a year.*
Dog Lady/Karen: *So you have custody of them?*
Me (unthinkingly/stupidly): *Of course.*

There is something in her easy unquestioning acceptance that adds greater weight to my sense of "day release" from grief and my role as widower of the parish. We have a great evening. She hasn't asked whether I'm divorced, widowed or whatever and somehow in that moment, for the first time since Helen died, it seems somehow not to matter. Later, as the pub quiz is announced, Karen grins and looks at me over the top of her glass:

Karen: *Do you fancy doing the quiz together? I'm pretty good at most things other than cars, books and marriage!*
Me: *Game on – those are my specialist subjects!*

She smiles and we embark merrily on the quiz, during which it is clear she has forgotten that she also knows bugger all about geography. As a team of only three, the hairy one of which is asleep under the table, we come a creditable third.

Later, drinks finished and pub pretty much empty, I get up to go.

Me: *I've got to be up early to get home tomorrow so better head back. Thanks so much for a fun time and nice to meet you both!*
Karen: *Yes, it's been great. Hang on. Look, it's a lovely evening, would you fancy a quick walk on the beach to*

give Honey a bit of a run before you go?

As I said, I like dogs and, indeed, liked Karen and so thought why not as the moon was up and the night surprisingly warm. In what follows, please assume that I have already placed a set of donkey ears on my head for my naive idiocy. I really didn't see it coming, nor my unintended complicity in what happened next.

Leaving the pub, we amble down the steps to a beach I have played on for more than 40 years. I'm relaxed and we chat, talking as we're walking. Honey bounds around us, happy to be out of the pub and looking for seagulls to chase.

Karen tells me about her marriage, her job and her sense of rebirth since her divorce and specifically how great it is to be sole decision maker again and free agent.

Reaching the pier she suddenly stops and turns to me:

Karen: *I've really enjoyed this evening. It's been all the more fun because it was so... (she struggles to find a word)... unexpected.*
Me: *Unexpected? How so?*
Karen: *Because I feel like doing this again...*

With which whispers, Karen steps in quickly and holding my arms as she does so kisses me full on the lips in a way that Auntie Ethel wouldn't recognise or like if she did.

What occurs next is seared on my psyche but takes so much longer to write down than happen:

Me: *No. No. No.*
Honey: *Yaaaaawooooo.*

Taken by surprise by Karen's cobra-like lunge at my lips, I spring back – it's been a long time since I snogged anyone to whom I wasn't married. Alas, in doing so I land on a brown doggy paw and it all kicks off.

Honey is upset and howls. Karen is upset and scowls. From nowhere I am sitting in the centre of a storm whipped up by a flustered, angry, rejected woman and an unhappy Labbie.

Karen: *What the hell! What's wrong! It was all so lovely. I'm sorry!*
Me: *I'm sorry. Sorry, Honey, Sorry. It was just such a shock.*
Karen: *Honey, are you all right? How hard did you stand on her?* (**to Honey**) *Poor paw!*
Me: *The sand is soft – it wasn't too hard. Listen, I'm sorry, it's just too soon. Too soon.*

There's a moment's silence with just the sound of the sea announcing its role as witness to this tragi-comic end-of-pier-show. Karen is crouching by Honey, soothing a clearly unhurt dog but slowly looks up and with an expression in her eyes hard to read by moonlight asks:

Karen: *What do you mean too soon?*
Me: *Helen, my wife, died a few months ago. We were together 26 years…*
Karen: *Oh God, that's awful. You didn't say! I'm so sorry. I*

thought you were divorced and when you didn't mention
an ex it did occur to me you might be a widower but I
assumed it was ages ago. You're so... normal.

I feel stupid but even guiltier at having not said anything
earlier to her about Helen but just for an evening I'd
wanted to slip out of my life in this special place. I feel
treacherous to Helen's memory, even if it's not late enough
for the cock to crow once, never mind three times.

With Honey happy, we walk back up the jetty and
she comes clean that her seaside snog had been clumsy
because she was *"out of practice"* but sincere and she had
gone for it because for the first time in a long while she
had wanted a bed buddy.

Karen: *It seemed the perfect moment to rejoin the human*
race. We'd got on so well all evening. You were funny
and relaxed and it all seemed bloody brilliant!

I wonder why I hadn't spotted her pass coming, given
the happy intimacy of the evening. Probably the
relative nearness of Helen's death played a big part in
anaesthetising me to Karen's fun and flirtiness. However,
there's something else, deeply unsettling, that in the
darkness has no name.

Later, pulse calmed and nightcap drunk, I'm sitting
drowsy and comfortable in front of the fire, trying to
work out what happened on the beach. It might have been
too soon after Helen's death in many people's judgment
but what slammed my brakes on was nothing to do with

bereavement and everything to do with more than 20 years of fidelity – I'd acted as a happily married man would, so of course rejected her pass.

Yet I'm no longer married and that deep unsettling feeling I'd felt afterwards has an explanation. It had been my libido raising its head for the first time in a long while. And now, thinking again about Karen and the near intimacy of our evening together, I think how fantastic it would be to share a bed with just such a kind, fun, sexy woman who has been good enough to tell me she wants the same.

For a minute I run happily, not guiltily, with the idea – I really would escape the widower script, hidden away from the rest of my life with its bedtime loneliness and never-ending bleeding logistics. It's not even about sex but a desire for flesh against flesh and a few hours of a world defined by the four corners of a bed and not a dishwasher or a washing machine.

Then again, how could I? How soon is it "normal" for a bereaved person's libido to wake up? Bluntly, how is it possible that a few months after his beloved wife's death a husband would have no guilt about wanting to shag someone? I don't know a widower or widow to compare timelines with and premature fornication is not the sort of topic you can dance into easily, even online.

Bereaved sexual reawakening seems almost taboo, with at least one brilliant exception. Marie, a supportive and close colleague, passed me Lucie Brownlee's *Life After You*.

Marie: *I thought this might help.*

Me: *Oh goody, yet another book about bereavement...*

Marie (lying through teeth): *No it's not about bereavement. I thought how many touch points you have with her, North Yorkshire and a frank view of the world!*

Me: *It's about bereavement, isn't it? The clue is in the title...*

Marie: *OK, it's about bereavement.*

Me: *Thank you.*

Marie: *Bereavement and LIFE, you idiot. Read it.*

Her intention was clear; she hoped Brownlee's experience would teach me something. And so it did when, glass of wine in hand late at night, I pulled it off the pile of generally depressing mourning material at my bedside and flicking through spotted the words "fantastic sex" on p190. This alone made it stand out like a beacon, as I say again, there is no greater taboo, it seems, for the bereaved than talking about missing sex.

I finished it before dawn and after the end of the bottle. This raw, brilliantly uninhibited story is about so much more than her libido awakening and the depths of her despair are waymarked at all times. It does provide details, though, on her fuck-buddy friendship with her plumber. That the reader ends up liking her more for it is a tonic to my spinning head. I'm guessing that as friends and family haven't disowned Brownlee, there's hope for me. Critically, her Carry On Plumber dalliance took place within the first year of her husband's death.

I worry, though, that while I'm technically single, to many of the people in my life, and Millie's and Matt's lives, I'm still married to Helen. So I'll tread carefully for their sakes.

For myself I find my lack of guilt at what Karen and I could have got up to a little upsetting and surprising, but not inexplicable. I loved Helen so much and would gladly have swapped places with her. While I scream out for more years together, there were no issues or unfinished business between us: we had something so special in the best of times and an even more profound love in the worst of them.

This helped me to embrace what may be the hardest lesson in bereavement – that you cannot love someone who is gone exactly as you did when they were alive. The contrast between the two states is too stark. I've understood this crappy truth quicker than many, perhaps primed by my dad's death when I was four.

So, no sex but also no guilt that there might have been …or could be soon. Bravado yet again perhaps, but I'm made bold and more open by Brownlee's honesty. You take help where you can through the layered complexities of this bastard bereavement.

The big lesson here, apart from if you are going to tread on a large dog do so on a soft beach, is that I now know that being a widower is basically being a sad single man with history. The ring is off and so are the gloves as I re-emerge as a sensual being, albeit one for whom everything is new and unformed.

Crazy, crazy new life. I long more than ever for the simple, beautiful old one.

18.

HOLIDAYING BY NUMBERS

B ack home warmer weather reminds me that I need
to plan our summer holiday and I'm faced with the
fact that the number three, so commonly seen as a lucky
number is one I've learned to hate with a black-edged
vehemence.

It wasn't always this way. Helen and I were an item for
years before our cosy couple became a fabulous threesome
with Millie's arrival, once sprogged-up friends had
finally roped us into parenthood with their rose-tinted
recommendations in our 30s.

No matter, the baby took our 11-year relationship to
a better place, and Millie was so lovely that we wanted
another. So Matt was born, and we went from "couple
with baby" to a full-fat family of four. It was brilliant: no
one's outnumbered, and there's a world of family tickets,
and board and card games that work well for four. No
disrespect to others with more or fewer children, but four
really rocked for us.

There came a time when the two kids really got on
and could play with and generally entertain one another.

This allowed Helen and me to reconnect. With hindsight, these were halcyon days when the sun beamed at us even if we didn't always feel its warmth so keenly at the time.

Then Helen fell ill and it was due to the beauty and bravery of the woman that nothing particularly changed in the happy gang of four, irrespective of medical treatment or darkening outlook. Nowhere was this more true than in holidays, although there was a heightened sense of *"do it now and screw the cost"*.

I absolutely love holidays but I hate going on holiday. Every aspect of planning makes me tense and the hell-in-a-bucket of airports, insurance, hire cars etc causes huge angst even with another adult to share the weight. Helen had, broadly speaking, planned the location, the timing and logistics of packing and I'd done the getting there, moving about and money stuff. The arrangement worked after she was ill as it had before, even if travel insurance for someone with fucking cancer became a deeply upsetting game of verbal fencing with idiots around disclosure:

Insurer: *Is her condition terminal?*
Me: *Meaning?*
Insurer: *Is she going to die?*
Me: *We're all going to die.*
Insurer (sighing but trying): *Sorry, has your wife been told that she is likely to die in the next two years from this condition?*
Me: *No.*

Technically I am being truthful but am aware that the

ice is thin and the song is long as I dance through the questions. In the end I found a specialist cancer insurer who knew their stuff, which included empathy and sympathy, albeit at a price. It took a while to find them – I say again, where's the frigging handbook for all this?

So in addition to Yorkshire, we had two fabulous family holidays in Helen's last two years. A road trip through Romania, staying most notably in Viscri, and then a full monty Florida trip – theme parks, alligator dodging, dolphin worrying and Anna Maria Island beach bathing.

The Romanian adventure was right up Helen's street, fuelled and eased along by the fact that my brother Richard lives there, and his wife Ioana worked immensely hard to make it special in our post-diagnosis world.

Florida was less obvious, Helen concluding:

Helen: *Wild horses wouldn't usually drag me there but I want to give Millie and Matt a holiday to remember.*

In denial, I didn't see so clearly that mentally she had inserted the word "me" after "remember", tragically aware this might be her last big trip. It was a very special two weeks in every way, even if Disney's best paled for Millie and Matt in comparison with two unrelated but very memorable incidents.

A constant factor connecting all the parks, other than sunshine, was the number of people on mobility scooters for the sole reason of their being morbidly fat. So fat that getting out of bed must have been a white-knuckle ride in itself, never mind going to the toilet.

Two such women parked in their scooters outside the Jurassic Park ride were at it hammer and tongs; wheel to wheel being the closest to face-to-face they could get. The backdrop to this conversation was most fittingly a ravenous looking T. Rex:

Scooter 1: *You're so fat, girl, you can't see your ass in the mirror!*
Scooter 2: *You calling me fat? Your ass is so big if he ate ya* (**pointing at Rex**) *it'd choke him.*

What was mesmerising was that both women held a huge roast turkey leg in each hand which they munched on between insults and panting for breath. Nothing we saw on the ride got close for memorability or mischief.

A couple of days later the excitement of swimming with dolphins was beaten in the fun factor by me being stopped by the highway patrol for doing 88mph. I totally missed seeing Trooper Dan parked facing the traffic in the central reservation but he didn't miss me.

As his cruiser pulled in behind us and he lit up the lights and sirens, the influence of hundreds of films made me want to floor it and head for the border in full *Thelma and Louise* mode. Instead of which I pulled meekly over, telling Helen, Millie and Matt:

Me: *Keep quiet and don't laugh, interrupt or contradict me no matter what I say.*

Slow talking, slow smiling Trooper Dan walked up to the car, hand on holster, before peering unfamiliarly at our international licences. Taking in the fact we were in bathing suits, in a rental car and sounding like David Niven (*"They really are complex and powerful, these American cars, compared to our small British ones"*), he decided, instead of issuing a ticket, to give me a demonstration of how to use the cruise control.

Me: *What speed should I set it at, Trooper Dan?*

I knew I was in danger of overdoing it. He looked at me quizzically:

Dan: *Well, on this highway 70 would be about right!*

By the time he left, I'd convinced him and pretty much myself that either I had a learning disability or back home I actually drove a Morris Minor.

Trooper Dan's parting comment made him the kids' friend forever. Walking off, he suddenly stopped and we held our breath as he turned back to our car and slowly and slightly menacingly put his head through the window:

Dan: *One more thing.*
Me (meekly): *Yes, officer?*

He looked around the car.

Dan: *The four of you. Be sure to stay safe, y'all.*

Another victory to the magic of four.

Our final short break together was my birthday weekend, which Helen kept secret for months. She maintained the subterfuge even into the Friday night journey:

Helen: *You'll need to drive without looking at road signs.*
Me: *Say again?*
Helen: *No looking at road signs. You'll spoil the surprise.*
Me: *But I'm not sure that's possible or lawful?*
Helen: *Go with it. I've kept this secret for months. I'll navigate.*

This was harder to do than you might think, and not recommended. After a somewhat adventurous trip, we arrived on a stormy waterfront facing what looked like a brick wall against a black sky. Helen was very excited, shouting:

Helen: *We're here, we're here!*

She was full of infectious gaiety as we stepped out of the car into a roaring gale like a scene from *The Tempest*. It was the Landmark Trust's magnificent Martello tower that I'd admired for so long.

The weekend was wonderful like no other and will be a lifelong reminder for me of how much Helen cared to make it special, including a surprise dinner in the tower cooked by her sister Sarah and brother-in-law Brian and waited on by our nephew Nathan.

One night the four of us watched *Casino Royale*, then, inspired by the film, we sat in the pub playing poker and comparing our "tells" – the unconscious body movements or speech patterns that show we are bluffing. For the record, Helen's was saying:

Helen: *Have I turned the iron off?*

Millie's tell was tossing her long hair, Matt's picking his nose and mine pulling hair from my ears (OK, so I'm going to be alone forever). I recorded this on my phone and it remains a poignant and treasured tribute to our happy card-playing foursome.

We walked, talked and generally loved one another; the 13ft-thick walls of the tower providing a temporary time out – respite from the stark fact of Helen's decline, as they had for so long from the raging Suffolk seas.

Indeed, so powerful was her life force during the Martello weekend, I'm convinced she saved her remaining strength for this final hurrah and expression of her love. Just over a month later, I was at her bedside as she slipped peacefully away.

With her death, four became three again, but a dreadful parody of the happy three of old. Three *sucks the big one,* as they say. Every card game, board game, table setting, ticket purchase and hotel booking shouts out that we are no longer quorate. Have you ever tried to play pontoon or poker with three?

And now I'm facing our holiday, our first as three, and I'm dreading it. Helen had been offered the use of a villa in Piedmont from a friend through work, but had not told me when, where or, most critically, from whom.

I am determined to go, however; this will be the last great salute to Helen's holiday planning. Luckily, at her funeral I had been saved from trying to profile the congregation for Italian home ownership as a tall mourner stepped forward to say:

James: *Hello, I'm James. Would you still like to come to Italy?*
Me: *Are you sure that is still OK?*
James: *Of course, we would love you to use it. Helen was very keen.*

Bereavement provides great insight into the over-whelming kindness of strangers. I would love not to have had the opportunity to understand this, but it's very life affirming, if ironically so. Kindness and the fact of talking about something so normal as a holiday that dark day made it all more bearable. It was a pointer to the future and helped more than James could ever have guessed.

Thus, it is with a mixture of joy and sadness that I book three, not four, flights for the first time, seeing Helen's now meaningless passport on the pile. I really hate the idea of just the three of us playing out an ersatz version of happy holidays past. Maybe it's macabre to think this way, but what would Helen have done if the situation were reversed? I imagine her in her Martello tower mode telling, not asking, me:

Helen: *If three hurts that much take a fourth person with you. Simple.*
Me (miserably): *But it won't be you.*
Helen: *Obviously, but how about someone the kids love, someone fun like Uncle Kenny?*
Me (more miserably): *But it won't be you.*
Helen: *Cheer up. Ring him now!*

So told, I'm on the phone to Millie's godfather, Kenny, asking him if he will be our "manny" (male nanny). Yes!

Our number flicks from three to four, and it all looks suddenly sunnier. We will blaze a trail through rural Italy, looking to the watching world like a gay couple with kids.

And so we did. Italy was great. A total focus on the kids, a new dynamic in having funny, kind Kenny with us, and I found myself really relaxing for the first time since Helen's death.

I know I was relaxed because while we were watching *The Italian Job* I experienced the same "Nooooooo!" reaction I'd had as an eight-year-old when the Mafia crush the E-Type Jaguars. On a scorching day in Turin we tracked down the route of the Mini Cooper's escape.

If I'm brutally honest, my ease was also because for the first time in ages I was holidaying without the worry of Helen's health and the emotional weight of knowing every second might need to be the stuff of precious memories.

Any guilt I felt about this sense of relief was

overwhelmed by the joy everyone took in the trip. This perhaps showed that I was turning a corner in dealing with the omnipresent weight of loss – imaginary conversations with dead wife aside.

I love that this sense of epiphany happened on a holiday chosen and planned by Helen, so perhaps even now she's still navigating me to sanctuary. Thank you, darling, wherever you are.

19.

HELLO ADAM

Back from holiday and reattached to the day-to-day logistical mayhem of our new life, I cannot help but keep thinking about Karen's beach kiss. I dwell on what might have happened if I'd not recoiled like a scalded cat and how surreal it was.

Every second of the whole episode is now frozen in time, etched into my memory, making recalling it easy. I find myself thinking how well it might work as a sketch in some grief-based comedy show in which the widower attracts the unexpected, the bizarre and the life-affirming like a mangy dog does fleas.

So I write it down. A lifetime spent in media means the idea of capturing ideas is an easy one, even if I was not myself a creative writer. To be fair, though, I'm reporting events, not originating them. As I get to the bit about standing on Honey's paw and it all kicking off, I start laughing at my own words and even challenge myself over whether this could ever actually have happened. Well, it did, even if once captured as prose it seems literally incredible.

Writing somehow helps me. I feel better for being able to examine, express and process events and so on I go, revisiting the early days and weeks after Helen died. Catharsis is a broad concept but one I understand better now as in the writing down, particularly of some of the moments of great grief, comes acceptance of the hard events described. What is self-evident, however, maybe also self-abusive, is that I enjoy reading my own stories, not least because the person in them seems to have a grip on things that their author simply doesn't.

Lacking confidence, I showed the Karen story to Pete.

Me: *What do you think?*

Pete: *I think you should have let her kiss you, mate.*

Me: *I mean would you read it?*

Pete: *I am reading it and you should have kissed her back.*

Me: *Is it any good?*

Pete: *Not for the dog!*

Me (loud and laughing): *Would you publish it?*

Pete: *Not unless you want people to think you are gay. No, seriously, mate… I think you're doing this for the right reasons but there could be unintended consequences – good and bad. It'll make you feel better. People who know you will understand how much you loved Helen and that this is the thrashing around of a recently broken heart looking for a way to deal with it. But* (**long pause**) *people who don't know you may think you are a heartless randy arsehole dancing on his wife's grave.*

Me: *So if in the unlikely event it was published and it was under a pseudonym, would that be OK?*

Pete: *OK. It's your funeral* (pauses, realising what he's said). *Sorry. It'll be fine.*

Helen had been an avid *Guardian* reader and we'd often commented that so many of the stories in the Family section felt familiar, despite being somewhat larger than life, but then I have always known from my career that fiction is rarely as creative as reality. My own stories felt fantastical but I was just writing down the facts with some sense of syntax and structure.

So it was that I searched out the e-mail address of the editor of the Family section, Harriet Green, and sent off two of my tales under the banner "Widower of the Parish". This description of me was the one I'd first used to church counsellor Ruth when summing up the sense of the heightened profile which partners my bereavement, welcome or not.

Sending a cold, unsolicited e-mail to Harriet in this way was spectacularly naive on my part. A newspaper column, it seems, is still a very desirable entity, despite the massive penetration of online blogs etc. Also I hadn't known of the 25,000 e-mails in Harriet's inbox and the very lean team running the section, who succeed so well by force of talent and experience, if not body count.

Two weeks later nothing had happened, which was a bit of a bummer and deflated my secretly over-pumped ambition. With somewhat jaded optimism, I sent her a cheesy but heartfelt second: *"It may have ended up in your spam filter..."* e-mail. In this I exhorted her to reply even if she thought my writing was crap; at least I'd know it had got through and wouldn't waste any more time writing.

Not long afterwards I was outside, using my phone to photograph, for the sale ad, my Princess Diana-era old Audi Cabriolet whose shabby-chic open-air motoring no longer matched my new Volvo-driving persona. Suddenly the handset started ringing with an unknown number. Tempting though it was to ignore what was certain to be a sales call, I'm glad I didn't. It was Harriet. After introductions she got to the point:

Harriet: *Thank you for these stories. They really are very good. You strike a clear balance between humour and emotion.*
Me: *Thank you. Thank you so much.*
Harriet: *Could you write 52 of them?*
Me (sitting down in surprise): *Yes, of course!*
Harriet: *Great! Well, let's start from April.*

And that was it. Looking back, Harriet, who is smart, vivacious and generally lovely, was brave to offer this, as I was a totally unknown entity. Even in her voice I could detect a sense of tip-toeing lest I burst into tears or break down as so often is expected of the recently bereaved. Standing up and looking down at the slightly arse-shaped depression in the Audi's bonnet, I felt elation of a magnitude I thought was forever denied to the bereaved. A red-letter day in every way.

Harriet had liked my suggestion of "Widower of the Parish" and suggested that I read the current incumbent of the column in the paper, Stella Grey, and her very funny and immersive "Mid Life Ex Wife" accounts of her online dating experiences. So I binge-read them all the next evening, glass in hand and head frazzled by the shark-tank world of profiles and posturing that she had so amusingly and successfully swum in. How glad I was not to be part of it.

I did have some disquiet, primarily that it was a bit daunting to have to follow her popular writing, but it was a new challenge and "new" is the drug of first choice for the meandering, purposeless bereaved.

Knowing Stella Grey was a pseudonym, I realised that I needed my own moniker. Although I would never write at all if being identified was a major issue, for the moment protecting the kids from any gossip which the column might generate so soon after Helen's death was important. So what to call myself?

Harriet rejected my use of my own Christian name and instead offered up "Adam", embracing my wider role as "everyman" – this made absolute sense and was not the last time I would take her counsel. The surname had been harder – like naming a child, you know that it's a big decision, the rightness of which will be tested over time.

A week or so later it's late and I'm still bed-dodging and in the final minutes of watching *Casablanca*, whose unchallenging familiarity should at least help me sleep. My intention of drinking less has not worked out so well and I start to ramble in the random staccato way of the truly drunk. Harry is the only non-judgmental, inscrutable witness to this poor show.

Me: *Ingrid Bergman. So beautiful. Dead from fucking cancer. Eva Peron, Beautiful. Dead from fucking cancer. Helen. Beautiful, Dead from fucking cancer. Audrey Hepburn. Beautiful, Dead from fucking cancer. Hang on!… Audrey Hepburn. Breakfast at Tiffanys. Holly Golightly. Golightly!*

I've always loved the name Golightly, so evocative of the film in which George Peppard tries in vain to keep up with the flighty beauty of Holly; the darker implications of Truman Capote's call-girl diluted for the big screen.

"Golightly" feels right. Familiar yet different and almost too great a fit. It's evocative of a life lived as a façade, feigning normality while moribund inside.

"Adam Golightly" sounds good-to-go to me. So good in fact it borders on being obviously chosen for effect and so a little pretentious. Gloriously, what I hope avoids this, at least to myself, is that Golightly is also a distant family name.

I googled to find that one Adam Golightly had been in court in recent years for stealing a 5ft-wide artwork from a gallery and making off on a bicycle. There's something surreal about this that matches my mood.

And so it was that Adam was conceived with Harriet as his graceful mother and me as hapless but hopeful father, aware that there might be unintended consequences of his birth but delighted by the chance to embrace them.

20.

IN LOVE IN-LAWS

Once I'd come down from the high of being commissioned by *The Guardian*, I realised that there were other stakeholders in Adam's story who needed to know, not least Helen's parents, Ray and Barbara.

"I haven't spoken to my mother-in-law for 18 months – I don't like to interrupt her." Ken Dodd's old joke rings hollow for me; I speak often to mine. It's a pleasure, though, to quote the newly knighted Sir Ken as I have always been a massive fan for his simple but compelling zest for life and it's so nice to have a childhood hero of my generation in the news for something lovely for a change.

To which point, despite some acerbic comments from Pete, I have not been able to face taking down the signed Rolf Harris artwork I gave Helen of her home city cathedral. It was a much-loved birthday present years ago when the Aussie entertainer's name held only the patina of childhood innocence. Now the pain of the painting coming down would be far worse for me than inciting occasional comments about the artist's deviance. There it is. I am still that raw; that brittle, it seems. Before Helen died, I'd thought myself tough. It seems this was *tough* as in toughened glass, such was the way grief shattered me, deeply embedding its blunt pieces to cause future pain when least expected.

Yet, for all this, I'm certain there's a sharper-edged grief whose shattering leaves more painful shards than mine. A grief I can only imagine and, please God, will never know.

I suspect there's a whole planet of pain in the death of a child that is so appalling, so damaging and so alien that unless you've been there you can never understand it. I think of this while reading tales of in-law angst on bereavement forums – "they hate me", "behaving badly", "asking too much", "interfering" etc. It must indeed be awful to have your spouse/partner die and feel that the in-laws are unsupportive. However, without being an apologist for people behaving badly, I wonder whether their difficult behaviour is because they're in a tunnel even darker than your own, and no less badly signposted.

Being older, one's in-laws don't have the distraction of young children to lean into and have less life left to rebuild. When there's also been a period of illness they may well have reconfigured their lives around their sick son or daughter and been left with a huge hole with little else to fill it.

The death of your loved-one-in-common kills the natural bonds between you and it will take time to form new ones. In that position I feel it important to think twice about burning bridges that I may wish to cross again in future.

But what the hell do I know? I've been lucky with my in-laws. In their 70s, when Helen first fell ill to fucking cancer, Ray and Barbara made a big decision to move more than 200 miles closer. Although retired for many years, they were still remarkably vital, with full, active lives supporting Helen, Millie, Matt and me through the storm of ill health.

Living very close, they saw more of Helen in her last 12 months than in the previous 12 years. Helen worried at first:

Helen: *They're putting themselves through all this upheaval just for me, aren't they?*
Me: *Bleeding right. Wouldn't you?*
Helen: *Of course.*
Me: *And your point was?*
Helen (laughs): *That you are a smart arse.*

She had understood and basked in their proximity if not the reason for it.

Their care and active support is undiminished by Helen's death. I genuinely love them and remain so grateful that they're here. Even though I don't call on them too often, the knowledge that I could is like a backbone that holds me rigid against incoming emotional and practical assaults.

The only cloud on the horizon caused by their proximity, one made a bit more visible and darker by my beach encounter with Karen, is that, whatever their expectation of appropriate widowed son-in-law behaviour, I know I am bound at some point to confound it in full view and so hurt them in a way Helen would hate. That it would then be reported through Adam's column makes this risk that much greater and their understanding, if not blessing of it, that much more important.

So I made a pre-emptive strike, sat them down, sherries in hand as liquid defibrillation if it was all too much, and started to share heartfelt truths:

Me: *In time I will do stuff that may make you raise your eyebrows and wonder just for a second: "How could he?"*
In-laws: *What sort of stuff?*
Me: *I've no idea what "stuff" means but it will include behaving in a way that I would never have done had Helen been here. When this happens please remember that I never loved Helen more than the day she died. That love and my grief will always be there, but to stay sane and be the person I promised Helen I would be for Millie and Matt, I need to build a new life around us. Helen encouraged me, but I want you to know too.*

I drain my own sherry and wait.

Nothing. Ray and Barbara didn't react. Shock? Upset? Rage? Hearing aids off?

Then, wonderfully, I realise it's a silence of understanding.

Emboldened, I continue to something a little more certain and edgy than "stuff":

Me: *Also I'm writing a weekly column for* The Guardian

called "Widower of the Parish". It'll be about Helen, me, us.

This caused if not a shock then an exchange of looks between them as if they were hunting to define the right reaction. This was clearly and understandably outside any reference point from even their long lives, and indeed still unlikely to my ears.

In-laws: *Will it be in your own name?*
Me: *No – I've chosen a pseudonym, Adam Golightly – it protects the kids from any unwanted attention and although it may of course get out, if it was a very big worry I wouldn't write it.*
In-laws: *Can we be called Ray and Barbara, please?*

And that was it. *Guardian* readers themselves, I'd had to tell them – how many funerals had "Mr Blue Sky" by ELO played live by a band of friends and family? It would have been very obvious. Both published authors, they found it easy to imagine me writing. They'd said little but this spoke volumes: they got it and, once again, I had foreseen storms where there were only warm eddies. So if I do end up writing up my howling at the moon or toasting the dawn full of life and libido I can do so knowing they still have my back.

Good on Ray and Barbara.

21.

ROCK BOTTOM
OF THE BOTTLE

It's September and a new school term beckons. Millie and Matt are apprehensive but ready to face the day. Their pose through the lens has them looking older, lovelier, smarter – perfect in fact. Just as the camera clicks a white furry face appears at the door, Matt shouts "Harry!!!" and the tableau explodes into blurred movement as we three reach for our gargantuan Siberian Forest cat making a run through the open front door towards the dangers of the road.

It's 8:20am and I'm capturing Millie and Matt's first day back just as I have recorded for posterity every year. This year matters more being Matt's first at secondary school and the first without Helen. Somehow their being clean and tidy in new proper-fitting uniforms and looking ostensibly happy is important to me even if Helen's sister Sarah has done so much to help. I'll look back one day to remind myself I was coping, at least as far as they were concerned, which ultimately is all that matters.

Matt hadn't been convinced:

Matt: *Dad, is this necessary? I'm not sure normal parents do this sort of thing.*

Me: *I'm sure they do, particularly on the first day. It's perfectly normal, thank you.*

Matt: *Well, they shouldn't. It would be better at the end of the day to show their kids had survived!*

I look at his deadpan expression to decide whether he's betraying nerves or simply being ironic. I favour the latter:

Me: *It's a big day, Matt, you'll not want to forget, hence the photo. That's all you need to know and in time will thank me.*

Later, kids happily departed, I'm alone in the kitchen, just thinking about getting dressed – but what for? I've taken the whole day off work to support them on what I'd thought, in error, might be a difficult one.

Instead it's me who's struggling with Helen's absence on this big day in our children's lives. I idly pick up the camera. In doing so, my sadness nosedives into a whole deep dark crater of grief. The deepest yet, in fact.

Thanks to smartphones, we use our digital camera rarely nowadays so the photos on it sit on its large memory stick for ages. Flicking through these pictures, I come across shots of a happy, healthy Helen from long ago. Looking at where we are on holiday in France, I realise these are pre-diagnosis snaps taken when the smiles and easy life within each montage are ignorant and innocent of the bomb about to go off among us. The blast would take Helen out of the frame entirely and leave us three survivors with potentially life-changing emotional injuries.

This was upsetting enough but I hadn't yet hit the bottom of the crater. The further forward I scroll, the less well Helen looks.

If the camera never lies it rarely gets to tell the truth this starkly as what I get is a fast-forward trip through her diagnosis, decline and death. Helen's hair gets thinner during treatment and then thicker as it grows back. Her face gets fuller with the drugs then becomes drawn, almost cadaverous as she loses far too much weight, her cancer killing her. Yet despite all this – the shock, pain, treatment and knowledge of her likely fate – in every single photo Helen, my beautiful brave friend, lover and wife, is smiling broadly. Her ability to see the best of everything undiminished by the fate she faced, she transfigures every scene with her joy in life.

It's the first time I've seen this sequence that runs like an appalling time-lapse movie. Changes that were incremental over many months are all there with the zillion-pixel sharpness of a modern camera. It's my lowest moment in months, which is saying something. The extra hard kick in the nuts lies in the photo of last year's first school day. Millie and Matt smiling with no sense of the heartache and tears that will land in their laps months later.

It's too much to take in and I do something I've never done outside of a stag weekend. It's 9:20am as I pick up the first bottle of wine and start guzzling it down without the intermediary of a glass. OK, it's not totally thoughtless; I know that Annie the nanny will be in later and the kids cared and catered for. It's not even like I get immediately pissed – the benefit of drinking too much for some months is that it takes more booze than it used to for the same effect.

Looking, bottle in hand, at today's shots, I notice how much older they look than last year and am hit hard by the knowledge that Helen won't now see them move into adulthood. It seems such an obvious point but I haven't clocked it so painfully before and it makes it all too easy to drink my way through to lunchtime. So it is nicely warmed up that I have my hand on the door handle of the local pub as it opens for business.

There I sit among the retired, beige-clad bar-room brothers and unwaged daytime tipplers. The beige boys are some of those whom Helen and I laughed about when we first came here as they'd often be found comparing medical histories with open folders containing graphic descriptions of their operations, which detail they were happy to provide to anyone with ears, such was the volume of their voices.

Beige Man 1: *Opened me up and it was the size of an apple.*
Beige Man 2: *Crab or Pink Lady?*
Beige Man 1 (triumphantly forming a large O with both hands): *Cooking!*

Helen and I had always come to this pub when we wanted to feel young again – like an instant makeover but with gin and beer. Today Helen's so visible to me in her absence, it's horrible and it does nothing for my mood when after a couple more draughts of beer I become not the audience for the old boys but the topic:

Beige 1: *Look's like he's had a couple already.*
Beige 2: *More than a couple!*
Beige 3: *Are those tartan trousers pyjamas?*
Beige 2: *No!*
Beige 3: *I think they are* (**then to me:**) *Hey, are you a Bay City Rollers fan?*

There's a pause until I realise they're talking to me.

Me: *Sorry.*
Beige 3: *Are you a Bay City Rollers fan – you know, with the tartan?*

To be fair, I'm wearing my "are they clothes or pjamas?" tartan trews and T-shirt, which are indeed pyjamas. I'm not, however, in the mood for banter and am pretty drunk on my self administered grief anaesthetic.

Me: *No, they're pyjamas.*
Beige 2: *PJs in the pub?*
Beige 1: *Why?*
Beige 3 (**to others**): *Told you!*
Beige 2: *Nah, you're a Rollers fan and too embarrassed to admit it, aren't you?* (**I don't reply.**) *Aren't you?*

Me: *Shang-a-Lang. Now piss off.*

Writing this down, it is all there. In actual delivery I suspect some of it was mumbled, bumbled and sporadically incoherent with possibly some dribbling.

I drain my glass and exit the pub, also leaving behind any memory of what I then did, where I went or how much beer I consumed. I suspect it was a lot, given how much cash I drank my way through.

My next memory opens with a buzzing. This wakes me from a very deep sleep. It's the alarm on my phone, which I always set to remind me to take over from Annie at 7pm. My head really hurts but through the pain I feel massive guilt. Today of all days I should have been home early to talk to the kids about their first day.

Opening my eyes gingerly, I find, terrifyingly, that my head is on a car steering wheel. Surely not? I look up in panic and glance blearily around. I'm in the driver's seat of my 1960s Triumph which I've had since I was 17 and which thank Christ is parked in my garage.

At some point I've come here with my Neanderthal brain's sense of self-preservation for a kip. The irony of it being the same car which has been a constant witness to key moments of my entire adult life is lost on me. More pressing are the facts that it is six feet off the ground on the hydraulic lift which I was using to fix it months ago and also that I've been sick at some point, largely down myself.

I clamber gingerly down and fortunately can change because there are overalls hanging on a peg below.

So it is that when I appear in the kitchen to take over from Annie I'm looking and smelling like a very down-at-heel Kwik Fit fitter.

The kids have had a good day and are happy – crisis, what crisis? Noting my odd outfit, Matt picks up the camera, still on the table, and points it my way:

Matt: *Your turn, Dad!*

I protest but with his usual quick wit and perfect recall he pins me to the spot:

Matt: *It's a big day, Dad, you'll not want to forget, hence the photo. That's all you need to know and in time you will thank me.*

Ha! It is true enough. I never want to forget or repeat falling into this well of extreme grief – a hard lesson on a sore head but one that has been well learned.

22.

KISSING MY CAREER GOODBYE

Annie the nanny heads off on maternity leave today and never were my emotions more mixed. She has been with us for 10 years, is a key part of the household and a source of care and continuity across pretty much all of Millie's and Matt's conscious memories.

After Helen's death Annie offered to move from three to four days a week, with the fifth weekday filled brilliantly by her sister Sarah. The scale of this support crew means that, when people ask, *"How are you managing the kids and house?"* and I reply, *"Fine"*, it feels as fraudulent as when I'm asked how much I'd enjoyed our first camping trip while calling to mind the joy of getting out of bed in the tent and going downstairs to the kitchen and bathroom, in what was the glampiest glamping tent (cabin with canvas roof) in glampland.

Organising a leaving tea party and presents for her and handing over confirmation of her maternity pay, I'm facing a future without her services with some trepidation. It is not on the scale of Carson's angst when redundancy notices were rumoured to be flying around at Downton, but I am worried about lack of support over the next few months.

My concern is not about the care, cleaning, cooking, laundry and chauffeuring that Annie does so ably – I can buy in some temporary extra hands and pick up any loose ends with the help of friends and family. What I cannot easily replace is her emotional support, personality and presence.

Matt put it with his usual razor-edged verbal scalpel:

Me: *Matt, you've known Annie since you were six months old are you OK with her going?*

Matt: *She's not Mum, but she's the grown-up woman I've seen more of than anyone and I love her. I'm going to miss her.*

Me: *You know, Matt, there's no certainty of her choosing to come back. She might not want to after having her baby.*

Matt: *You make sure she comes back, Dad, or I'll stay in my bedroom forever.*

So that's that, then.

Beyond that, here's a thought: should I be outsourcing parenting at all, even to someone as good as Annie? Don't I need to be around to see them off to school, be there when they return and help them with homework? In my head and without hesitation I see Helen nodding.

It is no more than I enjoyed as a child. My widowed mum worked full time. When I was very small I briefly had a nanny who'd been a massive Cliff Richard and the Shadows fan and I only remember her because I can picture her triumphantly holding aloft half a pair of black spectacles. This had been somehow separated from Hank Marvin's face when she and her fellow fans mobbed "The Shads" at Newcastle station.

From the moment I started school, however, firmer memories were formed. I never came home to a stranger. The difference, of course, between then and now is that my mother was one of 10 siblings. There was a tag team of relations, led by Auntie Eunice, to greet me from school and "be there".

It was my normal and I never thought there was anything odd about it – indeed there were many fringe benefits. Auntie Eunice, a Methodist, had no real under-standing of alcohol and lager was comparatively new in the UK when I was a child. After school there was a ritual that went:

Auntie Eunice: *Here you are – beans on toast as usual. Would you like* Blue Peter *on?*
Me: *Lovely thank you.*
Auntie Eunice: *Now what would you like to drink – tea, lemonade or a lager?*
Me: *Oh a lager would be nice, Auntie…*

Without that scale of support for my children, the obvious person best equipped to bridge the emotional hole left by Helen and then Annie's absence really is me. It's that simple. Whoever said that every day we make deposits in the memory bank of our children was, in my case, on the money. I can't make that happen if I am on a plane to the US or even an early train into London. Yes, the sooner I can take up and shake the reins left by Annie leaving the happier I'll be.

Even so, at my age it's no small thing to walk away from a big job because it's no longer what one wants out of life. Like a not-so-merry-go-round, once you are off it is almost impossible to get back on but I don't care because I've finally understood just what a wanker work has made me.

It was clear early on that one of the many unexpected benefits of writing Adam's column was being able to use it to test the water about plans I was making or as a confessional space when I felt I'd not behaved. Well, here goes – part of my need for change and why I'm so keen on loosening my hold on work to be at home more during Annie's absence is also one of the reasons why I still drink too much. It lies in the fact that I'm guilty of being a self-serving arsehole. How? Let's roll back to the weeks not long after Helen's funeral. I'm packing for a trip to the US and Millie isn't happy:

Millie: *Do you have to go, Dad? Matt and I miss you so much.*

Me: *Yes, I do. It's my job and it matters more than ever that I keep it.*

Millie: *Why more than ever?*

Me: *Because what do you think pays for everything now that we no longer have Mum's salary?*

Millie: *Are we going to run out of money, Dad?*

Me: *Not if I keep working, which is why I need to go away*
   for the week.

It's a scene that been repeated many times with variations
of *"I need to go because I need the job and we need the
money"* even when Helen was alive. Adding money to the
the list of worries feels like a low blow to a bereaved child.
But still I went, as I always went, with family caring for
the kids now that Helen couldn't.

Always a nervous flyer, I would sit in business class
quaffing champagne, fine dining and keeping an eye on
the engines. In the US, I would stay in swanky hotels,
indulging myself as self-justified compensation for not
being at home (a $25 bottle of bejewelled mineral water
in one of the Donald's tasteless towers comes to mind).

I am painting this vile picture because, after Helen
was diagnosed but was still well, I was treating these trips
like a mini-holiday from her illness. On one occasion, this
almost cost me the chance to say goodbye. I arrived home
on a Friday to hear from her consultant:

Consultant: *We worried that Helen could have died on
   Wednesday.*

This came from nowhere, and more hit and miss news
than maybe it should have been – I'd nearly failed to be
with Millie and Matt on the dreadful day as we flailed
around trying to understand and accept that their mum
was on her death bed.

Now, months after Helen's peaceful passing with me

holding her hand and talking of our love, I am still using the excuse of the facile crap of business imperatives to take time out from my grief and responsibilities. Why I see it now I don't know, but it is screamingly obvious and I hate myself for it. Before any kind, sympathetic soul thinks I've done nothing really wrong; this is not even the bad bit. When Millie says:

Millie: *We miss you, Dad!*

... she is sparing me the full truth of:

Millie: *We miss you, Dad, but we absolutely hate someone else having to come to look after us because it sharpens once again the pain of losing Mum!*

Every time I make a yellow-bellied retreat under the guise of work, am I dragging the kids backwards to the grief of their mum's death?

So complete is my sense of self-loathing that it makes the next bit a piece of cake. I'll never fly anywhere again for work or spend more than a couple of nights away from the children for anyone. Am I right or reckless to do this?

Hurriedly I organise a babysitter, allowing me a late pass to take my old friend Sally out for a drink to get some objective informed HR advice. I'd met her through her ex-husband with whom I'd worked and our friendship had survived their divorce. I had seen her once since Helen died when she had helped me decide how much time to take off and what was "normal" for bereavement. Sally is a senior player in my industry so speaks candidly.

Sally: *Clients won't make allowances, and your performance will suffer if you won't fly any more and can't make the meetings.*
Me: *I know.*
Sally: *They'll be sympathetic to your circumstances but you'll still end up with no job.*
Me: *I know that too.*
Sally: *Are you ready for the change? You're already over the hill age-wise as far as this industry is concerned. Big change!*

Sally was right, of course. But the harsh but brilliant truth about it is that I really don't care. Yet more bravado, but I really mean it. Fucking cancer's masterclass in life's fragility, my insight into my own selfishness and the kids' upset mean it feels right because it is right.

Counsellor Ruth looks at me wide-eyed when I tell her about my intention to ditch the job:

Ruth: *Your wife's died, you've bought a house, you are sweating it about your health and now are choosing to endanger your job.*
Me: *Yes, that's mostly the shape of it.*
Ruth: *Just how much more stress do you need?*

She sounds calm, but her eyes flash nutty-professor-scale *"are you mad?"*.

I'm not. The die is cast. I am learning not to fear change but embrace it as a means to carve out a new life, and a new sense of purpose surges through me. I'll nurture the kids to be the people Helen hoped for as I promised her as she lay dying.

As I help the now well-rounded Annie load her car with gifts and she promises to let us know when her nipper arrives, I am struck by just how much change the next few months and years might bring and I am learning to love, not fear it.

It is not by choice that I am here, but it is what it is.

Back at Downton, Dame Maggie Smith unwittingly becomes my spokesperson as she signs off the last episode:

Isobel: *We're going forward into the future, not back into the past.*

The Dowager Countess: *If only we had the choice.*

If only.

23.

HALF THE PARENTS
TWICE THE FEAR

I have never had that much time for TV but between faux tears and stage-managed "discoveries", *Who Do You Think You Are?* on BBC1 can strike pure gold.

In 2010 I remember being so moved when Jeremy Irons, pursuing his Irish roots, discovered and read so beautifully a poem, "Little Kate", written on Valentine's Day in 1857 by his great-great-grandfather. It was about his young daughter, and it moved me enough to scribble it down on the back of a bottle of Bordeaux that I still cherish, even though it's long since been empty.

It looks towards her growing up:

A winking blinking little thing full of deep-eyed witchery
Full of artless rollicking and ever busy as a bee
Making all the house to sing, she is the very joy to me
Waking sleeping early late my heart is full of little Kate

Ah would that time would leave us so
But she'll grow old and I'll grow strange

Content with loves that round her grow
She seeks not yet a wider range.

But years will come and years will go
And with the changing years she'll change
Then through the shifting scenes of fate
I'll look in vain for little Kate.

It's clunky but evokes the fleeting moments of childhood as lives expand and interests broaden. I'm so moved by its prophecy of regret at the loss of childhood personas and the comfort of having your children safely around you at all times. It's added poignancy lies in Kate being the sole survivor of the author's five children.

Millie and Matt were only 10 and six years old at the time of this beautiful reminder of childhood's transience but Helen and I had already long understood and embraced the fact that every moment of it is truly precious.

This awareness persisted even when we were right up against it in battling the logistics of busy lives and the physical exhaustion of young kids. We knew these were still great days, possibly even the best of them. I'd yack on as we flopped onto the sofa after a long day:

Me: *We'll look back on this as the most carefree time of our lives.*

Helen (tired after a long day at work): *How so carefree?*

Me: *Because they go only where we know they go and are in bed before us every bleeding night. But better than that they want to be with us! May not always be so.*

Helen, used to me banging on about loving the life you have, not the one you had or want, simply smiled. I hope it meant that she loved our life. I think so. I need to think so.

We had the usual child falling downstairs, broken arm on trampoline, scrapes and illnesses. Then out of nowhere a very bad thing happened to Matt.

Helen booked us into a historic building for my birthday weekend – a precursor to the great Landmark Trust Martello Tower – and Matt ran into the unlit barbed-wire fence that surrounded it within five minutes of us arriving on Friday night. It cut cleanly like a knife down his face, from just below his nose through his lip into his mouth. It was at the time the worst moment of my life against which all else was then benchmarked. We rushed to an unfamiliar hospital, where after a lifetime waiting with a bleeding, shocked small boy, I raged against the harassed casualty doctor's matter-of-factness:

Dr: *Yes, it's pretty bad but I'll have a go at stitching him up tonight.*

Me (looking aghast at Helen): *What do you mean "have a go?"*

Dr: *I haven't done many like this but it should be fine, with little scarring. It's such a clean cut – it really is just like a knife did it.*

I'd glanced at the nurse in whose expression I'd spotted some disquiet when the doctor had spoken, and asked her:

Me: *What happens if we wait until morning?*
Nurse: *We'd dress it. There's no need for it to be stitched tonight.*

I noted that as she spoke she looked at the doctor, not at me.

Me: *Then do you have anyone else who can give us another opinion tonight, please?*

After an eternity waiting a consultant took one look at Matt before declaring:

Consultant: *We're not touching that here. Can you bring him back tomorrow?*

So it was that Matt ended up in a different hospital having a general anaesthetic as the plastic surgeon put the tiniest stitches one could ever hope for in his face. He barely has a scar today. Thank you, Lister NHS Hospital.

Looking back, I know that sometimes I avoid confrontation and looking pushy but this underlined that as far as the kids are concerned every instinct to push and protect is ready for action at any time.

Afterwards we realised just how lucky Matt had been – a couple of inches higher and it would have been his eyes.

Of course we'd worried about the kids before but, as so many families do, we'd sheltered behind a belief that very bad things only happen to other people. The barbed-wire incident had dented that certainty and Helen's diagnosis and death destroyed its illusion totally. Now every worry I have ever had about the kids' safety has been supersized.

These fears are unspoken, usually unshared, but are unrelenting, making insignificant all my navel gazing over job, nanny, friends, sex, love, logistics and even my own mortality.

In starting to write for *The Guardian* as "The Widower of the Parish" I found myself as Adam Golightly being invited along to a preview of "Life. Death. Whatever.", a series of excellent events, installations and workshops with new and challenging thinking on death, grief and dying. Having wondered whether going as Adam was a good idea in case someone I knew turned up, I'm glad I did as it was provocative in a good way and my ego was stroked by a few people telling me how much they enjoyed the column. It was the first time in my life this has happened and it was a strange sensation as these strangers gave the impression that they "knew" me.

I met there briefly the founder of the Death Café, Jon Underwood. He seemed a modest and lovely man, whose movement lives on beyond his own sudden death from undiagnosed cancer in his early 40s, underlining the fragility and finiteness of life yet again. I didn't find the event or talks depressing at all, if anything they underscored that, since Helen died, I no longer fear my own death as I used to, other than as it might affect the kids. Instead, I have replaced any concern for my own mortality with a new scale of numbing terror of bad things happening to Millie or Matt.

This constant, shouty fear means I want to keep them

at home all the time. I hate them walking to school. I hate Matt's enthusiasm for rugby and fearless tackling. Millie and Matt both have black belts in karate but I still want to stand in front of them and take any of life's punches that come their way today and forever. I know all parents feel this way but it has become an unrelenting obsession of mine.

When I drop Millie at a teenage party, I stop myself waiting in the car for five hours, and being the least cool dad on earth. I find myself delighted they don't fancy horse riding despite living in a horsey county; my lovely colleague Jemma had a fall and broke her neck not so long ago and is now tetraplegic. It still gives me night terrors thinking about her accident and how death and injury seem to lie in wait everywhere.

I'm finally driven to share my fears with my counsellor Ruth.

Me: *Every parent worries about their kids but mine feels deeper. I'm worried as they get closer to spreading their wings that it's going to drive me mad or I'll behave in a way that stifles them! That's the last thing I want for them, or me.*

Ruth: *Your worries are no different to anyone's but your experience with Helen and even Matt's accident means you expect the worst, not just fear it.*

Me: *I do expect it. It's unbearable.*

Ruth: *If you're ever going to enjoy a normal father's relationship with his kids' growing up maybe you need help.*

Me (being thick): *Help?*
Ruth: *Get some proper counselling – not just me!*

There is sense in what she says and I will.

I remember reading one of the several copies of CS Lewis's *A Grief Observed* which kind friends had given me early on, in which he faces his feelings about his wife's death from cancer. It is less well known than his Narnia stories but was probably way more important to the poor bereaved man's sanity. In it he gives life to a thought that I hadn't really understood when I first read it, *"No one ever told me that grief felt so like fear"*. I understand now.

To avoid that knowledge driving me mad I make some enquiries that see me sitting in front of a counsellor, Andy, for what turned out to be our one and only consultation.

Andy: *It may be that much of your heightened fear is locked up in the fact that you feel isolated.*
Me: *How so? Do you mean lonely?*
Andy: *No…er… rather yes but not in the usual sense. You feel you are the only person of your age, background, family circumstance, wife's specific illness who gets it. It can be very isolating.*
Me: *That does sort of make sense.*
Andy: *I don't know whether you read* The Guardian *but there is a column, "Widower of the Parish", which might help you. The author has many of the same issues, although seems to be dealing with them better, perhaps because he has been bereaved longer.*

It was not the only time this happened but was the first time I'd paid to hear it.

From that point I didn't believe in Andy but I do believe in counselling so I, not Adam, will search on. He doesn't need it apparently!

24.

FAILING BY FALLING
FOR JO

"Kindness is a language which the deaf can hear and the blind can see." – attributed to Mark Twain.

Well said, but Twain omits that kindness makes your head spin when it's from a smart, single, spectacularly attractive woman and you're a grieving middle-aged bloke.

I'm sitting at my friend Jo's kitchen table in her house in Scotland. I like her company a lot.

She didn't know either Helen or me previously, finding and accepting me as I now am – never looking over my shoulder or tap-dancing around my bereavement. I found this so refreshing from the very first time we met when Matt was invited to her son's paint-ball party. Hair tied back, in bulky, baggy clothes and without any make-up or jewellery, she'd come across simply as "nice" if slightly shy and scatty. She was so naturally smiley that I'd found myself ridiculously disappointed when having offered to give Matt a lift home afterwards, someone else had stepped in. This feeling was OK though, I rationalised; it was not as if I found her physically desirable. I just liked Jo a lot which on first acquaintance as an adult so rarely happens, least of all to an introvert like me.

That very first evening I'd e-mailed her thanks for the party and for sorting the lift and we'd started a virtual conversation. This was memorable for two very different reasons. Somehow I mentioned the fact that I'd just bought the cottage in Yorkshire, only to discover that her mother had owned one less than five miles down the coast and her childhood summers had also been spent there – possibly not all the same summers as she was 11 years younger than I was.

It created a ridiculously fast-track connection between us, augmented by the second fact that every one of her e-mails that night was signed off with "xxx".

Now I come from an industry where everyone kisses everyone else and in personal texts a "x" is just a friendly currency with "xx" reserved for when you really mean it. "xxx" on early acquaintance had no precedent and threw me. My 26 years of being out of the game gives me a naivety regarding the opposite sex that must seem semi-comical, although not to me then or even now.

Jo and I became friends and I realised that those first impressions, other than of her friendliness, were absolutely wrong. That charming scattiness was overlaid with a quick, sharp intellect and a very accomplished character both professionally and personally.

Divorced for many years, she offered me excellent

advice about raising children alone. Indeed, she has a single-mindedness about not just coping but making their lives richer that was inspirational to a widower wading in his loss. She had no time for fools or things that were uninteresting or diverted her from her demanding profession or boys. This made her easy kindness and friendship even more touching.

And friendship it really is, offered with a naive and delightful lack of awareness that – as the town's most eligible divorcee – being linked with its most recent widower might have led some people to paint her scarlet if they believed she had amorous intent so soon after Helen's death.

She had no such plans even if the circumstances we found ourselves in were the perfect setting for undisturbed clandestine coupling. We were alone in her lovely large house in the furthest reaches of the middle of bleeding nowhere in Scotland. My recently purchased townie's 4x4, a second-hand Volvo, had at last faced challenges greater than the kerbs in Sainsbury's car park and was parked outside in the darkness, happy to be covered in mud as never before.

Jo's invitation to stay and my acceptance was known to no one, it was "time out" in the best sense of the word. I had gone there firmly and happily in the friend zone, hard though it is to stay there when she raises her head from the Aga, raven hair sticking to her flushed face, blue eyes sparkling with the enthusiasm that so characterises her and still on her knees makes me the sort of offer I love:

Jo: *Fancy some homemade crumble? With custard?*

Could we ever be more than friends? Thinking this, my head starts spinning and not simply because of the strong Innis & Gunn beer she favours.

In Adam's column I'd already identified and shared my lack of guilt at my libido kickstarting itself in Yorkshire but this is something potentially far more treacherous. It wouldn't be wrong for me to fall in love again, of that I am certain, indeed Helen and I discussed it, but surely that timeline is measured in years, not months?

Even assuming Jo was interested, what sort of impact would that have on Millie and Matt or would it have to be a secret for ages and therefore be something shabby, small and doomed?

Even though I'm sure that none of this is vaguely on Jo's agenda, I really like her, the first fresh acquaintance in my new life who is female and single – one whom I instinctively like and who for reasons I still don't understand seems to like me. We get on well. She comes round and joins us under the duvet watching *Prison Break*, lusting with Millie after actor Wentworth Miller. She banters along as we josh about whether she really has a horse-woman's backside which while not true becomes a running joke. Another way of looking at it is that she offered an easy adult female familiarity with us that the kids had not enjoyed since Helen died. Hence a dark cloud blew over our house when she decided to move:

Me: *I'm afraid Jo's moving away to Scotland for good.*

Millie: *Oh. I like Jo. She's mad but fun.*

Matt: *Mainly mad.*

Millie: *That's rude!*

Matt: *I like her too.*

Me: *So do I.*

Millie: *Because she likes* Prison Break?

Me: *Despite that.*

Matt: *Why don't you ask her out?*

Me (closing dropped jaw): *Do you know what that means?*

Matt: *Of course.*

Millie: *Yeah, Dad, ask her out.*

Me: *She's a friend. She's moving to Scotland.*

It's surprising even with hindsight just how easily Millie and Matt accepted that I could like a woman who was not their mum enough to want to date her. More extraordinary that they should suggest it! The kids continue to surprise and delight me and as they are the only audience whose opinion I truly value, that really matters.

It's still way too soon, though, after Helen's death. The theory that patients fall in love with their doctors is well known and I wonder in my self-aware, navel-gazing way whether I'm responding to her kindness in that model. Only time will tell. I am certain that had Helen not died I wouldn't have noticed Jo, but then she would not have made contact – another bleak, virtuous circle.

Parking the ramblings of the emotionally stunted 12-year-old that I seem now to be, Jo has a stellar career yet is so successful in raising two fantastic boys. That in itself provides hope for successful single parenthood and hope is what I need.

There is a ridiculously heavy statue in my garden (a birthday present for Helen) of Pandora, whose box, once the evils of the world were released, held only hope. It's what's left and what keeps me sane on bad days now I've almost (not really) banished the bottle. Seeing Jo's living testimony to how well a single parent can inspire their children to thrive is psychotherapy without the couch. Even though her wild passion for life makes me wonder what she'd be like on it.

Enough. This is something I need to deal with. My connection to Jo was hard forged in the extremity of my grief and will probably survive time and distance.

With her I've felt happy in a way I'd thought gone for good and not entirely because of her fantastic apple crumble and custard.

I don't want to alienate her with the sort of unexpected and ill-delivered pass I've been on the receiving end of myself. How would I deal with it if she started screaming, slapped me or worse still, kissed me back?

Even after thinking all that, sitting on my surrogate sibling's sofa drinking, chatting and laughing late into the evening, I wonder what would happen if, legs curled beneath her like a cat, Jo leaned in to kiss me. I think I know the answer, and looking over her shoulder into the deep darkness of the Highland night, I expect to see hooded figures carrying flaming torches and pitchforks as Helen's friends, family and my more judgmental fellow travellers on grief's journey get wind of my thoughts.

To be honest, though, given that it's only a few months

since Helen died, I might have joined them.

All: *String him up!*

That night, lying alone in my bedroom at the other end of the house to Jo's, who I assume is cosily tucked up in her four-poster, I am laden with angst and deep frustration. Were it filmed, fans of *Witness* would recognise my expression as that on the face of Harrison Ford a few feet but a thousand miles away from Kelly McGillis in the bedroom across the corridor. Between Jo and me are 30 feet of squeaky floorboards, Iona, her prowling black wolf-like Alsatian and the likelihood of shocked rejection. I go to sleep. Good decision.

There's no doubt that I was drawn to Jo with such a powerful, visceral surge of positive emotion that it caught me unaware, coming as it did so soon after Helen's death. Foolishly I didn't understand that it was the very fact it was so soon which drove my battered, bereaved, uncounselled psyche into full search mode. This left me looking for love with open arms but also, as I was soon to be shown, hungry to hate with burning, barely suppressed anger.

25.

First Fight Fright

I've parked and am walking through the DIY store car park towards my appointment with a tin of *Eating Room Red*. I have been motivated to make sure the house keeps intact happy memories of Helen but does not become a shrine. Decorating and new doors will underscore the rebuild of our lives as I choose to make changes instead of just coping with them. This vision does require posh paint, though, and lots of it. Easy thoughts of colour and cost are meandering happily through my mind when I'm suddenly called to stark attention:

Voice: *Oi! You just nicked my parking space! ... Oi! I said you just took my fucking parking space!*

I realise that the owner of this aggressive accusation, a bloke in his early 20s, girlfriend in tow, is addressing me and I go full-on middle-England peacemaker:

Me: *So sorry. I didn't see you, but you've got a space, OK?*

I gesture towards his newish-looking sporty Vauxhall. With possibly suspect assumptions on my part about its value and noting that he was fairly well dressed, I didn't feel any threat despite his tone.

With hindsight, I was a bit thick. I could and should have been more aware that a combination of my smarter, if older, car, his girlfriend watching and probably the fact I'm older, shorter and bespectacled made me a soft target for shouty boy's hard intentions.

As I walk past he reaches out and, grabbing my shoulder, spins me violently around using his superior weight and height to good effect.

I've never really been in an adult fight despite years of karate with the kids. I remember the martial arts teacher, our Sensei, stating clearly early on that, more than about fighting, Karate is the art of running away with menaces – reacting only to aggression and seeking as few blows/actions as possible to disable your opponent so you can remove yourself from danger.

Sensei: *Always look to avoid conflict, assuming that once you commit you will end up either in hospital because you failed or in court because you succeeded.*

Tough stuff, we pupils thought, reflecting the fact that while a fun family activity on a Saturday morning, karate is also an all-in and very vicious martial art that would have the Marquess of Queensberry spinning in his grave. I've never used karate despite six years' training with Millie and being awarded my black belt when she won hers. That I do now was a surprise and testimony, as if I needed it, that something bad can happen out of nowhere.

As he spins me around I put my fingers into a knife hand position as I have done so often in training, then carry forward the momentum he has created to chop him in the side of the neck. This was rather harder than I intended, which was very hard indeed, but augmented by his own violent motion.

I had been remarkably calm and careful, though, remembering Sensei's warning:

Sensei: *Make sure you contact the side of the neck, never the front or you'll crush their windpipe and kill them. The side will be enough to disable them, allowing you to leave.*

He's right, it was enough but I don't leave. My would-be assailant, his own fist raised ready to smack me in the face, crumples silently and immediately to the ground. I'm a bit shocked that it worked but still cool and calm.

Then the really frightening bit happens.

My calmness vanishes. Seeing him lying there, I'm overcome by possibly the greatest rage I've felt in my life. Looking at his inert form and face, I want to follow him down to the ground and really hurt him. That he's down there doesn't matter, it's fair game in karate but the fact is I want to press home my attack on his eyes, nose, face and bollocks with my feet and fists. Doing so would break every oath I've taken and would probably have me locked up.

He is saved by his girlfriend. She starts screaming with the volume of a shrill town crier:

Girlfriend: *You've killed him! You've killed him! He's fucking dead! You've fucking killed him!*

Her words are like an ice bucket challenge over my seething, uncontrolled anger. I still don't run, though, as concern overcoming caution, I stick around to check he's OK.

It's a dicey decision; it could all have kicked off had he got to his feet. Then the situation is defused once again by his girlfriend who, on seeing him open his eyes, proves that nothing is predictable in relationships. She starts shouting again but this time at her now groaning beau:

Girlfriend: *You arsehole, Warren, you picked that fight and got what you fucking deserve. You were already parked when he arrived. Wanker!*

He is clearly OK physically, but under siege of a different sort, so I say goodbye, hop in the car and leave the paint for another day, not wanting to find a reception committee waiting when I come out of the store or the car in component form.

Anyway I've much more to think about now than decorating with upmarket paint products however smoothly they go on. I'm a bit shaky about the whole thing. Actually that's not true – I'm in pieces over it.

It shows how things can turn in a second – he could

have knifed me – what then for the kids? More than that and potentially almost as disastrously for them was the crazy level of anger I'd felt. What might have happened had Warren's girlfriend not brought me to my senses? The last thing the kids need is a dad charged with ABH, GBH or worse.

I consult my friend Hamish; employed as a civilian by the local constabulary, he makes the point:

Hamish: *How many times did you hit him?*
Me: *Just the once.*
Hamish: *That's OK then. More than once and you'd be in trouble for sure if there's CCTV there and he went to the police.*

That is some relief but I'm really worried. It was as if his action had given me not only permission to defend myself but step right outside the boundaries of normal behavior for the first time since Helen died – a chance to go nuclear and let my feelings rage against a world in which tossers like him are alive and Helen isn't.

Friend and agent provocateur Pete probes further when I tell him how I'd felt:

Pete: *Fighting! Seriously?*
Me: *Nah – that was a one-off. I didn't look for it.*
Pete: *Tell me then what you would have done if she'd not been there or if the kids had been there and he'd threatened them?*
Me: *I would have killed him.*

I shock Pete but shock myself even more as I realise just how primed I am for violence. If he'd threatened the kids I'd have happily seen him dead and somewhere in the darkness of the moment would have enjoyed it. This isn't me or certainly isn't who I was but the need to defend Millie and Matt, that any parent feels for their kids, is so amplified by Helen's death. It is the very reason why amateur counsellor Ruth suggested I needed professional help.

Me: *I need to chase the counselling, don't I?*
Pete: *Absolutely. It's a warning and you got away with it but only just. You should send Warren's girlfriend flowers – she saved you. Spend less time worrying about decorating and writing all this balls down for your column and get that counselling sorted NOW!*

I may have needed this to happen to drive me on. He's right about how close I'd come to disaster and could so easily be again. If life is a board game I'm lucky to have been dealt a CHANCE card reading "Get out of jail free".

26.

WINDOWS ON HELEN'S WORLD

Holly: *If you could say one more thing to Helen, what would it be?*

Holly is a daftly insensitive but well-meaningly crass cousin. My answer comes straight from the heart, surprising me and shocking her:

Me: *I'd tell Helen how much better I understood her job, how good she was at it and how loved, valued and respected she was by so many of those with whom she worked.*

Holly looks at me, wide-eyed:

Holly: *Is that it? What about that you loved her, the kids, how you are coping? Her work? Reeeeaaally?*
Me: *Really.*

I'm suddenly tired of the conversation and reach for another egg-and-cress sandwich. Why do these taste so much better at funerals? My aunt Grace, aged 93, is the last of my mum's nine siblings to pass.

All 10 lived heartily well into their 80s, except Uncle Fred, whose health one assumed was fine until he crashed to earth in his Lancaster bomber aged 21. So I'm here with regret but no grief. Helen's death in her 40s has created a new benchmark that has anything above 60 looking like a good innings.

With the six siblings on my father's side long gone, it truly is the end of an era as the aunts and uncles who were so much a part of my life are now absent. With what I suspect is a common sense of regret, I wish I had spoken to some of them about our family history before they died, not least my own mum who may not have been certain what day it was at the end but could provide forensic detail about the distant past.

Later, on the long drive south, I play back and unpick Holly's question and my unconsidered reply. Helen and I were always so close, never more so than in the last two years. My time at her bedside as she slipped away meant that, when she died, there really was nothing unsaid between us, or so I'd thought at the time.

It was only when preparing her eulogy that I had been prompted to consider her career as never before. I remember being bowled over by some of the quotes from her colleagues, including Dame Fiona Reynolds, formerly of the National Trust:

Fiona R: *Helen was so principled and clear; she always had something valuable to say and she carried the flame of the Trust's core purpose so strongly.*

There had been people of influence and standing at her funeral who'd worked with Helen professionally. Some of these I had not even known she knew, never mind respected her well enough to come to her funeral. After the service I greeted everyone, including a tall, distinctly patrician gentleman introducing himself:

Man (hand outstretched): *Geordie.*

I was momentarily tempted to ask whether he'd travelled down from the north-east that day, to thank him if so, but instinct stopped me. Later from Helen's boss I had confirmation that the instinct was a good 'un, Geordie was better known as George, Earl of Carnarvon and owner of the fabulous Highclere Castle whose upkeep has been so helped by its fame as Downton Abbey.

I didn't cover this in Adam's column as it made me uneasy to mention individuals so soon after the funeral but do now as Helen would be happy for me to point out that since not every house can be featured on TV it's up to us all to support Britain's unique heritage. Visiting historic houses, castles and gardens means we keep alive our history while ensuring their future relevance. This was Helen's vocation, her passion and something I now really understand she was truly skilled at and a cause I support unequivocally. It's why it's OK to sound like some of the above came out of a brochure – it did, one that Helen wrote.

This new understanding of Helen's professional persona made a big impact on me at the time and obviously still does even if I now wish I'd embraced it harder and earlier. It is a bit preachy, but why not open wider your own wife's, husband's, partner's work window and get a better view – you might learn to love them more while you have the chance to tell them why. Meanwhile, I had some wonderful news from her boss Hugh:

Hugh: *It's not in the open yet but it's been agreed in principle that we will create an annual award in Helen's memory for all the outreach and education work that was so important to her.*

I was thrilled, as were Helen's family. Most importantly its annual presentation would create for Millie and Matt an enduring window onto their mother as a passionate professional, not just an adoring mum.

And now I saw another way to create a long-term reminder for the kids of their mum, *actual* windows of the stained-glass variety.

Years ago, Helen commissioned a leaded-light stained-glass panel for her parents' 50th wedding anniversary. It is a lovely thing, beautifully crafted and painted by Tony, who, operating out of a small unit on his family's farm, produces glazed and leaded masterpieces.

Gazing at the window in Ray and Barbara's house, I have a sudden and rare brainwave – to brief Tony to do some small stained-glass panels celebrating Helen's passions.

The longer I live with the idea the more exciting it becomes. I can engage immediate family in the brief for each of the small panels I'm hoping to install above the front door. Here they'll be an enduring reminder of Helen, a more accessible memorial to her life to complement the slate memorial in the churchyard but without any need to visit that beautiful but sadly sepulchral place.

So it is that the children and I are back briefing Tony on the five little windows. It is a poignant moment, slightly spoiled by watching the kids hopping around amid so much sharp glass in his studio that I'm wondering whether I should have put the local A&E into the Volvo's sat nav.

We had whittled down the many things Helen loved, including:

Millie: *Playing cards, Yorkshire, the art deco cinema down the road, Christmas,* Some Like it Hot, *Family get -togethers…*

Matt: *Harry Potter, picnics, first snowdrops, poppies, her Inspector Hound children's stories, old films, long walks, holidays, the zoo, the Abbey…*

I am struck that the list has nothing of that big part of Helen that I have had brought alive to me so recently – her career in the heritage sector, the greater understanding of which made me a little more proud, a little more in love, and her loss a little more dreadful.

It is why the final list for the window paintings is:

- **Inspector Hound** – her as yet unpublished children's book character
- **Durham Cathedral's Knocker** – historical signifier of her place of birth
- **Hogwarts Crest** – she loved reading Harry Potter books to the kids
- **Art Deco Light** – from the Rex cinema that was her last outing on earth
- **Knebworth** – historic house she loved, whose owner was her friend

The briefing went very well with some lovely, life-affirming moments for Millie and Matt, even if for me spending so much time thinking about what Helen loved had high-lighted for me the extent of how much fucking cancer had stolen. A grief ambush. I kept it together for the kids on the day even as I was knocked to the ground emotionally. There is an episode of Inspector Morse where John Thaw reflects on the fact that he would regularly go and start the engine of his ill friend's car to keep it charged. The second that friend died, however, this ritual lost any sense of purpose or intrinsic meaning. For me now so many of the activities or objects that Helen loved are either joyless or upsetting without the focal point of her personality and enthusiasms.

How often do I wish that fucking cancer's cup had passed us by and landed on some other poor sod? How loathsome am I for thinking it? Were the column a film it would have faded to black for a while as I ducked revealing in print that for a short time Adam had slipped headlong into grief's dark hole accompanied only by bitterness and booze, but still no tears.

27.

THE O' TOOLE SANCTION

I had often taken strength during periods of unexpected upset from the humorous and surprisingly positive tweets of my work colleague Jemma who, after nearly dying in a riding accident, spent months, now years, dealing with and fighting the fact of tetraplegia. She railed against the darkest matter-of-fact diagnoses of consultants and has made great inroads into getting movement back into her arms and body. She can drive an adapted car, does sport and has even started fundraising for the good causes associated with her accident.

I am not sure that I share her strength but have been inspired by her endlessly, even in the rare times when her own conviction and courage seemed to have wavered:

Jemma: *I would like a weekend off now, please!*

I understood that cry so clearly, the desire after so long being seen to be getting on well and coping with all the crap of a new paradigm, to have a break from the reality of the present, and find myself back in the old less challenging, less "always on and coping" life.

That her next tweet was back to her usual positive form lifted me too.

She might also be surprised to discover that sitting alongside her ready for action on the bench of my personal inspiration dream team is Douglas Bader.

Matt bought me a book about RAF hero Bader. I have always found him fascinating, a man defined but not constrained by the accident that resulted in the amputation of both legs. I still love the story David Niven recounted about Bader giving a talk to an upmarket girls' school, and describing the German planes attacking him. It goes loosely:

Bader: *...I had one of the fuckers behind me... one of the fuckers in front...*

This prompted the pale-faced headmistress to interrupt with:

Headmistress: *Ladies, the Fokker was a type of German aircraft.*
Bader: *That's as may be, madam, but these fuckers were in Messerschmitts!*

I would love the story to be true. Many years ago, I spent a week filming on a Scottish hillside; three of us having dinner each night with actor Peter O'Toole. On the first evening, ice unbroken, I told him the Bader story and for all his own many, many tales he hadn't heard that one and hooted with mirth before reaching for another one of the three bottles of red wine he drank over dinner. His laughter created a connection that made it easier over subsequent nights for me to discover that he had regularly visited the seaside village in North Yorkshire that I now own a house in, staying in the local pub and playing cricket on the beach with his son.

On the final night, after he had performed an impromptu snippet of a scene from the play *Jeffrey Bernard Is Unwell* on a barstool in the local inn, to a bemused but friendly audience, he pulled me to one side and whispered in my ear in a way that suggested no time at all had passed since Bader was first discussed:

Peter O' Toole: *Bader's stumps made him mentally stronger than his enemies and gave him a physical advantage in the air. With legs, you'd probably never have heard of him. Tragedy can grant gifts...*

Young and star-struck, I wrote it down; I had little idea what he meant but time has plugged the gaps and I do now.

Bader's accident had made him mentally robust and determined not to be cowed or constrained by anything; his glass was always full. It wasn't all psychological, though, as he was helped by the fact that his heart had less body to pump blood around, so he could perform tighter turns in a dogfight without the risk of losing consciousness.

For me, knowing that loss is now and will always be my brother is tragic but emboldening and therefore empowering. Grief's gift means that I have no fear of change, or the decisions that change demands. I am not at full power yet, being still constrained by what are still early days of shock and realignment, but I'm en route. Physiologically I have no need for an "edge" to shoot down aircraft but I am more aware and more determined to be fitter, faster, stronger and live well and longer.

Reminding oneself of a multi-Oscar-nominated actor's words is an unusual way to deal with grief's darkness but alongside Jemma's sparky courage it lifted me back into the daylight.

So successful was it that I shrugged off an awkward conversation with my colleague Roger about my growing sense that my job might be best relocated to the US since I am so reluctant to travel.

Roger: *If it does will you relocate?*

I looked at him wide-eyed, taking a moment to take in what he was saying.

Me: *No chance. It's the last thing the kids need and in truth I'm done with it.*
Roger: *The client?*
Me: *The industry.*
Roger: *What about the money, the experience, the status... your age?*
Me: *No. Done with it. I want something new that allows me to be more present for the kids and will see me into my dribbling dotage.*

Roger (in tone that implies I'm mad): *Er... OK. If you are sure.*

I am. Mindful of O' Toole's words, I might now be a grief-hewn master of change. I should have been brave enough to break away and try something new ages ago but was never brave enough to jump ship. In fact I'd still enjoyed the media world, even if my seniority now meant I did less of what I love. I also enjoyed the cash and the perks; but for me, as for so many poor sods, it was fear of change, of taking that first step in another direction, that locked me in. How many people are stuck in jobs this way, ones they no longer love or tragically, never did love?

That's why being made redundant with its forced change is so often a driver of ambition and personal growth. Someone else has taken the decision and hope-fully paid you to "go for it".

The world of work will never look the same to me. Through it I now see employment as renting out bits of my precious, beautiful but short life – no money is worth something you no longer love. Bereavement is dreadful, but once you accept that the life you had is unrecoverable, you might just be able to create a new one that isn't simply the old version but sadder.

Reinvigorated, I focus away from loss and back to the positives of the present. Briefing John had reseeded my love of traditional stained glass into the more fertile soil of this new life so I decided to go on a taster course in Scarborough to learn the basics of making it.

I was lucky. These courses are very popular and with

only four students at a time are booked well ahead, so I called with little hope. Hurray, someone had dropped out that day so setting in motion a series of fortunate, inspiring and potentially life-changing events.

In Scarborough I met Dawn, with whom I worked side by side creating our first pieces. The work itself – designing, cutting and framing the glass and lead – I found straightforward and surprisingly easy. Dawn was a bit older than me but we got on well and with her husband Richard went that night to Alan Ayckbourn's Stephen Joseph Theatre. It was the revival of one of his 1980s plays, with Ayckbourn rather wonderfully sitting behind me still looking to fix things that he was unhappy about 29 years after its premier. Now that's passion for your job!

I had noticed during the day that Dawn seemed to be struggling physically and there was something in her appearance that echoed for me in a bad, sad way Helen's time on steroids. Sure enough in the bar:

Me: *Are you coping OK, you seemed to be struggling a bit with all the standing?*
Dawn: *I was. I've got cancer in my spine.*
Me: *Oh God, I'm so sorry, Dawn.*
Dawn: *It is a shame* (**she shrugs**) *I'm probably into the last few months now.*

I'm poleaxed; moved and inspired and, not standing on ceremony, share Helen's story. As I do I see in Richard's face a shift in how he looks at me; no longer just a new acquaintance but someone who has already travelled the journey he is on, someone still standing at the end of it. I hadn't really understood until we spoke the importance this sense that a surviving partner can still have a life is for those who are living with a loved one with a life-limiting illness.

I hope I helped him in some tiny way as I valued meeting them both so much. Dawn's story was the final push I needed to start to re-engineer my working life and therefore my personal life. This much I now know – the two are not separate in any way.

Just as Helen never stopped her piano lessons or enthusing about the people and passions of her very full but receding life, Dawn is here on a course to learn a new skill simply because she enjoys it despite her illness. Both are extraordinary and reach out and remind me that the privilege of good health is a gift, but one that cannot be assumed. So applying my new-found willingness to embrace change, as soon as I return home, glass panel in hand, I decide to approach professional stained-glass man Tony and draft a letter asking simply whether he has a vacancy for me to work with him, so becoming probably the oldest stained-glass-window trainee in the country. This would complement my keyboard time writing the column and no doubt provide new content to report as Adam's new normality fleshes out. I do not send the letter immediately, only because I need to know when my job will transfer so I can commit if he says yes.

I hope this hesitation is not weakness. I can't allow these new opportunities, legacies of Helen's love, to be shot down in flames by the sort of fear of change that would have overwhelmed the old me. I need courage, conviction and the sort of good old-fashioned bloody-minded bravado of which Messrs O'Toole, Bader and Jemma would probably approve!

28.

BEDSIDE BLACK HOLE

Imagine Narnia's evil twin; a place of darkness without talking animals or the gentle Aslan. It's a place overseen by the grim reaper and his more terrible sidekick, fucking cancer.

Entry into this bleak world is not through a wardrobe, although it is via another piece of bedroom furniture. My bed is a thing of beauty. Purpose built some years ago by a bloke in a Dickensian-looking East London workshop, the brief to the surprised-looking designer was *"like the one in the film* Bedknobs and Broomsticks, *but in stainless steel, please."*

Despite the lack of a magical knob, I've discovered that it can transport me back through time – unfortunately that time is the dark hole of despair when Helen died.

The very night of her death I started sleeping on her side of the bed because the clock is there, and once the move was made simply continued to do so and although I retire late, I always sleep well. One night much later, slightly worse for wear after an afternoon clearing out her desk had me take comfort in a bottle of Merlot, through long-established instinct or muscle memory I moved back to the side I'd occupied for so many years. It was a shift of three feet (it's a big bed) but I might as well have thrown myself onto spikes.

When I looked across to the empty space that had been Helen's side, my sense of loss was overwhelming. I shut my eyes, but the spikes dug deeper. I remembered what it was like to wake beside her for so many months, wondering whether this would be the day the pain started getting worse, the test results more negative or, in the latter period, seeing her ever-thinner body taking up less space under the same duvet.

Like the drunk whose world starts spinning when he closes his eyes, I start to feel waves of despair crashing into and breaking through the defensive wall which has kept the deep dark hole of grief at bay and allowed me to maintain the façade of "coping so well". This despair is like nothing before, lying at the very core of me, it is as black as a winter night and as I find out when I try it again sober, unrelated to alcohol.

This new bedtime torment I explain to Heidi, my recently recruited, very professional and calm counsellor. I know nothing at all about her and she gives nothing away. Cheery enquiries are met with a stonewalling professionalism:

Me: *What are you up to at the weekend?*
Heidi: *I really don't think that matters.*

I am surprised at first but it works, providing a rigour

to our time together that contrasts well with the overt concern and open-ended sympathy of church counsellor Ruth, lovely though that was and is.

I signed up to 20 sessions in a small room off the high street, furnished with two comfy chairs, a fan and an ominous and immense box of tissues at my side. Heidi is dark-haired and on first acquaintance seems quite conservative and I wonder how well she will maintain her calm when I unload on her stuff not all of which I can believe is typical of a relatively recent widower who desperately loved his wife.

In fact I need not have worried as Heidi listened to all that and much more as the weeks rolled on and events took over with barely a flicker of changed expression. She could take the shirt off your back at poker such is her professional deadpan demeanour. To date only this bedtime "discovery" and my informing her at the first session that I was writing the "Widower of the Parish" contemporaneously with her counselling have registered any sense of surprise. Her "tell" in poker parlance being a shallow, short intake of breath and a slight body move. Even then she cuts straight to the chase with a key question:

Heidi: *OK, so are you here as yourself or as Adam Golightly?*
Me: *Myself. Adam is fine.*
Heidi: *Why are you here? Are you looking for absolution for your behaviour or help to overcome your loss?*
Me: *I hope the latter. I'm like a high functional alcoholic – seems fine but isn't underneath. A "griefoholic" perhaps.*

I want counselling to insure against any meltdown in the future.

She doesn't smile and indeed rarely does. She also steadfastly does not read the column while I am a client even when she knows that she features. She is, in short, bloody marvelous and exactly what I need.

I'd entered into these sessions thinking that talking about myself for an hour to anyone would be good to flush things out but Heidi is brilliant at teasing out the truth, not just the "smiley coping" with which I have laminated my broken heart. She also quite early on did help me live with my crying crisis:

Me: *I'm also worried that I never cry and have not done so since Helen's diagnosis with fucking cancer.*

Heidi is unflinching at what to me is a massive confession which I think makes me somehow lacking in some understanding or acceptance of grief:

Heidi: *Maybe accept that you may never do so in the way you think you should. Grief has many channels to express itself, not just tears.*

It was tremendous to hear, although the fear of a meltdown still lingers but further back in my queue of concerns. Not crying has been one of the reason I drank so much – partly in an attempt to provoke the drunk's maudlin tears – so at least my liver gets an early break through counselling. For all this good stuff, though, I sense my marital bed observation is a new one for her as she probes gently:

Heidi: *What happened next, as the despair got worse?*

I'm not sure what she expects – that I died? Was sick? Took up crystal meth?

My answer definitely challenges her poker face, her eyes flash momentarily with shock mixed with incredulity and there's the sharp, shallow intake of breath and the slight adjustment to how she is sitting, which for Heidi is the equivalent of me dancing on the table:

Me: *I just moved back to Helen's side of the bed. Everything immediately returned to normal. Grief gone. Solid walls of coping back in place.*

Saying this out loud makes me realise that this must sound crazy but I've repeated the move several times since – shifted sides of the bed in a maelstrom of despair and then moved back and been immediately fine without even a lingering upset.

So, once again, my life reads like some cheesy film script in which the inexplicable becomes the everyday.

I hadn't reckoned, however, with Heidi.

Heidi: *OK, tell me why you really moved to Helen's side of the bed.*

I don't reply at once. It's a good question and needs thinking through – it would have been just as easy to move the clock. I'm exploring long-buried memories:

Me: *My dad died when I was four and my mum told me she chose then always to sleep on his side.*

In counselling terms, I suspect this hits pay-dirt as I continue:

Me: *She took over the family business a week after his funeral and coped extraordinarily well with three children under 10. She understood coping.*

Heidi digests all this and does her stuff. By the end of the session I'm pretty sure that I'm following a bereavement survival strategy imprinted since childhood. Even my seeking counselling, despite northern instincts to be a strong, silent type, is because my mum had none. This caused her depression and a drink issue later that I wish to vanquish in myself. My mum's story really is one of angels and demons and is even now guiding my own.

So after only a few of Heidi's counselling sessions grief's deep dark hole, which I'd always feared was out there waiting for me, has been identified and hopefully with her help can be managed. That the gateway to this black place is my own bed is unexpected, but not so much as my ability to move back to Helen's side and be immediately fine.

This is big news if only I can learn to face the darkness

and understand it better. So it's with enthusiasm that I start to spend longer on the far side of the bed; like someone training for a marathon with ever-further runs. Each time the deep dark hole threatens to swallow me, I return to safety and sanity by moving back to Helen's side. That this works again and again is magic and tragic, two words probably familiar to CS Lewis, whose writings I have turned to before as the closest thing I've found to a handbook to grief. He understood in 1961 what I understand now through Adam's column, that to write about grief really is to start to cope with grief.

What I am also discovering, courtesy of Heidi, is that to talk about grief to someone who knows their onions is even better than writing and worth its weight in gold, never mind a very reasonable £30 a session!

Heidi has given me great confidence in the benefit of counselling. When hurtful critics on Twitter, always themselves bereaved and on a different journey from mine, throw bricks at Adam, I am able to recommend counselling with a genuine belief in it. Their anger towards my version of loss is indicative that their own remains unresolved.

I wished them well and hoped they'd find their own Heidi; mine was very much taken.

29.

KIDS' FIRST CHRISTMAS AFTER MUM

I absolutely bloody love Christmas. I really do. Presents, pantomimes, tinsel and trees, every ritual fills me with elf-like glee. So people moan about the commercialisation, blah blah blah, but it's CHRISTMAS!!!

I sometimes wonder whether my own love of the season stems from the fact that my dad's unexpected death when I was a small child was on Christmas Eve and as a family we sought to compensate with extra festive cheer. Certainly my memories are full of massive lunches with a house happily chokka with aunts, uncles and cousins in various degrees of getting a little drunk, watching the Queen then a Bond film or *The Great Escape*.

Helen loved it even more than I did, which is saying something, with her own childhood memories of big family get-togethers. In what turned out to be her final Christmas, less than two months from her death, Helen's participation in treasure hunts, laughter games, quizzes and general festive frolic over dinner was undiminished even if she could eat little at that late stage of her illness.

With hindsight she was so frail and thin, her life force must have been massively strong for her to be still so central to the season. I remember her sitting there on Boxing Day evening, so full of happiness surrounded by family. Smiling, she gleefully ranked her favourite Christmases and thankfully, given what was shortly to take place, that year was right up there.

Even with this back-story and knowing Christmas is generally always coming, I am shocked when two days before Halloween Matt chirps:

Matt: *Look, Dad! It's nearly Christmas!*

He points towards a tree twinkling merrily in a window.

Me: *It's just a tree with lights on, Matt.*

My reply dismisses his discovery too quickly, so challenging Matt's youthful determination never to be wrong, which desire triumphs over his equal determination never to walk a step faster than needed, as bounding up the final steep steps of Whitby's surprisingly named Khyber Pass, he reaches the tree pointing:

Matt: *Look, Dad, it's got a bloody fairy on top!*

Reaching the car, I make a mental note to watch my swearing in front of Matt. The much bigger, darker note, though, is a new weight on my shoulders because Matt's tree has highlighted the impending reality of spending our first Christmas without Helen as our festive cheerleader.

I had been worried about work and this new worry did me a favour. There is a myth that to offset the pain of injury, you can pinch yourself and focus your mind elsewhere. But how far do you go?

As Pete observes when I point this out to him:

Pete: *You don't need a Nobel prize, mate, to know that if I cut my finger and you kick me in the balls, then I'll forget all about the finger.*

The fear of team Golightly having a miserable Christmas without Helen has without warning totally overshadowed the worry that, by Christmas, the words of Wham Rap, *"I'm a soul boy, I'm a dole boy"*, could apply to me.

At work, my unwillingness to travel for the kids' sake has come home to roost as my boss Philip calls me into his office:

Philip: *I'm afraid there are some issues on how well you are coping with the role operating from Europe. They've decided to move your job back to the US.*

I had expected, indeed hoped, this would happen as a consequence of my no longer being prepared to travel or go the extra mile in any sense but it is scary, even with the generous terms on offer.

This may mean the end of my career, as I'm not prepared to work the long hours again while the children are at home and I have rather run out of steam anyway.

Helen was diagnosed two weeks after I started this job and in truth the whole role, company, client and maybe industry has been tainted for me by association, certainly for now, probably forever.

My employers have been great, though. They've behaved in a way that suggests they really are a "people business". My tell-it-how-it-bleeding-is colleague Roger questions my seeming lack of concern:

Roger: *Aren't you worried you'll run out of cash and have to sell the house?*

Rather wonderfully the answer is simply:

Me: *No.*

Perhaps selfishly and certainly pretentiously, I subscribe to the thought attributed to Dostoevsky, *"The soul is healed by being with children"*, so I'm looking forward to spending more time with the kids and can park money troubles until a point in the future when my own soul is perhaps less frayed.

As for Millie and Matt, the idea of my income plummeting, with a reduction in what we can afford, is I hope offset by the fact that they will see more of me.

My intrinsic optimism as a person is remarkably undiminished by events and I believe that by putting myself out there workwise, good things will happen around me. I can now formally approach stained-glass Tony about working as his trainee, pressing send on the e-mail written but not sent a few weeks previously, after the Scarborough course.

Shoulders back once again, I start planning the best Christmas possible. It is what Helen would want. I'll take my lead from George and Andrew on this one: *"Make the most of every day. Don't let hard times stand in your way."* Whamtastic!

Taking cheesy 1980s tracks as a mantra for life has often worked for me. The pathos of doing so being supercharged with hindsight, given George Michael was approaching his own "Last Christmas".

I found that writing the column about my fears for the emotional pinch point of the big day shone the sun on the mists of my worries and pretty much burnt them off. I'd hoped writing might soothe the general rawness of my grief over the long term but this was near real-time embrocation of a specific immediate woe. Extraordinary.

So comes the big day with Millie asking as she has done so often, face glowing with Christmassy enthusiasm:

Millie: *Dad, why is the Ooh Ah bird called the Ooh Ah bird?*

Me (lying): *I don't know.*

Millie (squealing with delight): *Because it lays square eggs of course!*

She, Matt and I laugh uproariously at the well-worn joke from the *1977 Good Life Christmas Special*. We love watching Jerry, Margo, Tom and oh-so-sexy Barbara (my pre-pubescent crush lingering on) in this episode "Silly,

But It's Fun". This has been part of our festive ritual for many years. Margo's Christmas order is not delivered:

Margo: *Jerry, Christmas is cancelled!*

They go on to have a simpler but super day with their lovely self-sufficient friends next door.

This year is the first time we have watched it without Helen but we are OK. Better than OK. In Yorkshire at the new cottage by the sea, we're living my vision of a place of sanctuary. Helen's family are with us and this gives us more than enough critical mass for games and a general busyness that holds upset at bay.

So far, it is working. Coming to the village that Helen knew and loved risked emotional seasonal meltdown, but the cottage is new to us and we are laying down memories of a new life without her physical presence but with us so much in memory and especially in Christmas spirit.

Indeed, half close your eyes and you might think Helen was still here. With Millie and Matt and we adult kids so excited there is little silence but is does feel that Helen has just popped ahead. Far from being upsetting, I find it quietly reassuring, so powerful is her presence. We're in a good place in every sense, accompanied by laughter, optimism and joy.

This is the easy Christmas. I suspect we are all in shock and next year will be the acid test. Helen's aunt Lillian sent me a framed Emily Dickinson poem, "Hope Is the Thing", which I had shuddered at because for me hope seemed defeated by death.

Now I get it, and in a Dickensian inversion, we are all loving Christmas Present, comforted, not haunted, by Christmas Past. Christmas Future? We'll be OK.

30.

FINDING A FUTURE HISTORY

Back home for New Year, and there's a scattering of Christmas cards on the mat which were posted late – I have no issue with this as my own are usually shoved in the letter box on Christmas Eve in personal triumph that the pre-festive prep is over and I can start to enjoy it.

One of those received I can declare is the outright winner by a country mile of the "Christmas card sent without thought" competition. The envelope addresses only me but the card adds "…Helen and family", along with a chirpy, handwritten message: *"Have a fantastic Christmas and best New Year ever."*

It's not from a close friend but they were at Helen's funeral. It's low-key hurtful, but short of going round there and giving the fairy some company by shoving the Christmas tree where the sun doesn't shine, there's nothing to do.

Their crassness is symptomatic of manic busyness but the card prompts thoughts in a mind tired by many motorway miles about New Year's Eve and every other New Year to come.

In qualified terms, the message is right. Any year that's not the one in which your wife died of fucking cancer has to be an improvement. "Best ever", though, sets the bar rather high, even if I'm grateful to have made it this far with the people I love seemingly sane and as happy as anyone could be dealing with the loss of their mother, daughter, sister, friend, colleague.

And I *am* looking forward to New Year celebrations, despite the fact that it'll be the first time in 27 years that I'll not kiss Helen at midnight and look forward with her to a shiny, sparkly, brand-New Year.

We'll be with some of our closest friends whose support and love has survived the loss of Helen, the more outgoing, sociable and generally nicer one of us. I'll probably drink too much and gabble a bit to offset any latent gloom but will be fine come midnight.

I'm sure my being upbeat is not bereavement mania but based on rational thought. I explain to my counsellor Heidi:

Me: *However crap this year's been, nothing gets close to what Helen dealt with every day of her illness, and my loss pales beside hers in absolutely everything. Being miserable is a bleeding indulgence.*

Heidi is unconvinced.

Heidi: *Adam, you are being emotionally fundamentalist,*

you've every right to be miserable.
Me: *For sure, but frankly I've had a bellyful of being miserable. It's not who Helen was, nor who I was or now am.*

I'll never get over the screaming injustice of her death and the rawness of it is unappeased, despite a head full of the need to nurture the kids as sole adult-barely-in-charge, liberal applications of alcohol and the distractions of ending my job, buying a house, fast cars, fighting, a national newspaper column, raging libido and generally being busy. But I can, as smarter people than me say, try to move on without leaving her behind.

I've talked this through with WAY (Widowed & Young) member Andy, the only person I know in my situation. His wife died a year before Helen and he has a steady girlfriend, new job and well-balanced kids.

Andy: *Give yourself a break. Being widowed was not a vow of hardship or chastity, a commitment to being alone forever or a punishment. Create a new life that'll make you happy and make the kids happy. Anyway, they'll leave home in a few years, you'll be alone, and by then so old and wrinkly no one will fancy you!*

More tough love but speaking from his direct experience of the worst happening, Andy's encouragement rings true.

I do now know that I'm pretty crap without a partner, confidante, lover and friend. I appear like someone who is coping well but while not hollowed out, am woefully incomplete. I've lived most of my adult life, indeed most of my life, conjoined to Helen – and without her my emotional wellbeing is running on fumes.

I'm not sure when and how I might find someone but on New Year's Eve I'm acutely aware that the person who has most closely filled that space in the past year won't be around.

My friend, sister-in-loss and definitely non-lover Jo in her friendship, lifestyle, common sense and white-witch-like sensuality has helped me not just stay sane and survive but actually thrive.

She filled a hole with her basic kindness and appealing idiosyncrasy. I've turned her way like a shrivelled flower does to the first rains after a drought. We walk late at night with Iona, her wolf-like dog, the darkness making it easier to declare my love for her as my sister-in-loss. She'll be the last person I text this year and the first next and she'll call en route north tomorrow as she makes the move to her holiday home in Scotland permanent. The legacy as she leaves is the knowledge that I haven't emotionally atrophied.

As midnight approaches, it's with a sense of sadness, of course, but also with a resolution to run faster – not away from life but at it, arms open, lips puckered, head up ready to embrace the best of this beautiful world for myself, for Millie and Matt, and in doing so, for Helen.

Writing this up for the column made me question as never before whether "The Widower of the Parish" was becoming more than just a record of feelings and events but might actually be driving my behaviour. I don't mean

I have been actively looking for column content but that by thinking about how I will report the future I have been consciously and more importantly subconsciously steering myself towards it. This is the "visioneering" so beloved of life coaches.

I've always preferred the Muhammad Ali version – his *future history*. Before a boxing match he'd spend days and weeks picturing the day of the fight in every detail from getting up in the morning to knocking down his opponent. He did so with total commitment and belief, naming publicly in pre-fight press conferences the round where the knockout would happen. This was much to the dismay of opponents, as many times he was right.

It is possible, in fact probable, that writing about Adam is helping define how I feel and how I behave. I was so determined that the New Year would be a good one that I am certain it drove the sense of positivity and successful weaving of happiness around Millie and Matt.

Whatever its provenance, this potent sense of purpose carried me through the celebrations and Jo's sad departure and into the first few days of what is still a Happy New Year.

It sees me having a cheery early-year curry with Pete, who's definitely not enduring a dry January.

Pete: *So, what resolutions this year, mate?*

I ponder – this year no one has asked. Why? Possibly because it's too risky a question for someone whose last two years have been burned by the death of their mother, then their wife, and who is facing the next one without paid employment.

Lose weight, drink less, be kind to people, get home earlier, etc, are resolutions I've spent a lifetime avoiding. They fade to grey quickly and become tributes to the resolver's lack of willpower rather than what lifestyle magazines describe as "New Year, New You" achievements.

Just before Christmas, I caught Mona Siddiqui's Thought for the Day on Radio 4. Her piece was beautifully written and presented, being about life, death and AA Gill's early passing in particular.

M. Siddiqui: *Death, like love, gives weight to our lives, it helps us appreciate what is important and makes us grateful for simple and ordinary days.*

The thought of death giving weight to our lives speaks little but says everything to a bereaved person, who will measure it against their own story.

For me, this weight has an imperative – an over-whelming recognition that we should never postpone happiness, love, good deeds or anything that matters to the future. If we do so, it is unlikely to happen as planned, or, if unlucky, at all. I put this "weight" thought to Pete as we chomp through poppadums before the main course. He ruminates for a while.

Pete: *As I see it, it's extraordinary that we sit here eating the equivalent of two bags of crisps before our* *dinner and think it's normal.*

This wasn't the insight I'd been hoping for but I don't underestimate his instinct for an offbeat prologue followed by a diamond-tipped drilling into an issue.

Pete: *You've been recalibrating normality – not just to a future in which you're OK without Helen but to the thought that you might have a new life as fantastic as the old one. The weight for you, mate, is not that the future could be bright but that you'll feel guilty if it is!*

I stop chewing and stare at him, questioning but calm. To those unused to Pete's caring nature, this link between Indian appetisers and my beautiful late wife might seem crass – but it's the man, and doesn't offend.

He munches on:

Pete: *Also, your survivor's guilt has been getting worse, not at being left alive but that you might waste that privilege. What's happening now is these two forces are meeting, with the fear of failing to create a brilliant new life for you all now being greater than the fear of the guilt if you succeed. So you can evolve.*

Pete winces, for dramatic effect or because he's accidentally gone for the lime pickle:

Pete: *People hate change but it can take you to great new places, and your change was one of the biggest possible.*

Helen wouldn't object to that new place being brilliant for you and the kids – that's what love is. Live it large this year, swing that weight and always choose the jalfrezi, not the korma.

I'm not sure if my lay life coach's curry-based counselling makes total sense. But his permissive and upbeat call to spice things up stokes my New Year's positivity. There are 51 weeks to go, but at last I will dare to dream and most importantly, to actually bleeding "do"!

To which point and returning to Ali's *future history* for a moment – it really is life coaching meets sports psychology but such is the genius of the man it precedes them both. Where the former often fails, though, Ali didn't because he also understood having a vision is nothing without accompanying bloody hard work. He would get up earlier, train harder and hone his talent sharper than his adversaries:

Muhammad Ali: *The fight is won or lost far away from witnesses – behind the lines, in the gym, and out there on the road, long before I dance under those lights.*

Adam and I are a long way from dancing under the lights but we are both certainly now on the road even if on this occasion he runs slightly ahead of me. Maybe all of us rebuilding after grief need our own *future histories*. There's a thought.

31.

SEX! TESTING THE TABOO

The scene opens as do my eyes on the early light of a grey day. I'm screamingly aware that my bedfellow is neither one of the kids nor Harry the cat. Patently it's not even my bed. Looking around the unfamiliar room, I cannot help but notice that lying beside me, leg thrown over mine, is a blonde-haired woman who has either avant-garde skin-tone PJs with pink spots or is as naked as the day she was born.

I stare at the ceiling in both shock and an unintentional tribute to Billy Crystal's pose from *When Harry Met Sally*, when he wakes up to the horror of having slept with his close friend, played by Meg Ryan. Without too much stretch of the imagination, it is fair to say that we have spent the night together, and with full consciousness comes great guilt at my first sex since Helen's death. I burst into inconsolable tears, crying like a baby.

So runs the script, but not the truth. I don't wake up at all because we've not been to sleep, having spent the night, as Keats wouldn't say, "hard at it". Better still, or massively worse in the view of a few of my fellow widows and widowers whose grief is more immobilising, it was absolutely bloody marvellous.

Far from guilt, I feel like the bloke in the classic film *Ice Cold in Alex,* longing for a cold beer while enduring days in the desert, who finally gets to lift the icy glass to his lips. Well, I've been lifting warmer things to mine in the last few hours and do so again, so missing two of the trains home that the more restrained, bereaved version of me should have boarded.

I'm a long way from home at a college reunion in the north of Scotland after much haranguing from my friend Tom:

Tom: *Come this year. You're not working, so no excuses. I've been asking you for years. Bloody come!*

I've ducked these dinners on the basis that the fellow students I liked in the past I still see – they're called friends – but the rest I wouldn't choose to travel up my garden path to meet again. Harsh but fair. More dubiously the mantra "hated them then, hate them now", I think, is a good one. However, Tom and his wife Gail have been kind and supportive since Helen died and I agree to go.

As it turned out, I really enjoyed the reunion's chat and camaraderie; my senses sharpened by low expectations and, I suspect, the sheer relief of a night off from my widower cares and relentless practicalities.

Over dinner, by chance or by Tom's unsubtle hand, I'm sitting directly opposite Lucy – possibly the only single woman in the room anything like my age in what is a very male-dominated environment. I didn't recognise her at first but she was not such a stranger and if one peers at my graduation photo Lucy stands an arm's length behind me among the ranks of many hundreds of smiling, optimistic, unworn faces.

After a slow start, we get on well. We had not taken the same course but there was still enough common ground to kick things off and ease my way into chatting someone up (is it even still called that?) for the first time in 27 years. We are getting on like a house on fire in a giggly, daft way.

Then the killer question comes:

Lucy: *So do you have kids?*

OK, so not the "married" question but maybe my lack of wedding ring answers that.

Me: *Yes, I have two kids at home, which makes being away all the more of a treat.*

Cheesy but stay with me on this, it really had been a long time:

Lucy: *So they live with you, not their mother?*

Momentarily, I'm tempted to lie, claim to be divorced as I know how being told that the man they'd previously quite fancied is a widower works like a bucket of Harry Potter's Polyjuice potion transforming any woman instantly into my concerned mother.

But I'm not Judas and won't deny any facet of Helen's life or death. So I pour cold widower-water onto the rising heat of Lucy's interest:

Me: *No, I'm afraid my wife died last year.*

Even as I say it, the words sound really odd. I hadn't distanced Helen's death into another year before.

The effect is also new; Lucy is moved but not maternal. She shares much of her own back-story of marital break up and many years of career focus and relationship voids. We talk long and late, connected by our own versions of adversity. Later in the hotel bar it seems like the most natural thing to kiss, protected as we are in the bubble of the moment. Lucy is unwilling to go further, however much the attraction of our reacquaintance.

I'm really enjoying myself. When she tells me that she doesn't think we should sleep together I don't know what to say and have no pre-prepared "lines", so fall back on the truth:

Me: *Fair enough. I can promise bugger all in the way of commitment anyway as I'm only going to get a chance to come here once in a blue moon, given the childcare situation. It would have been lovely, though.*

I smile cheekily, almost without agenda. I really am just talking the truth and in this as in most things it either attracts in its sincerity and candour or affronts in its lack of sensitivity and polish.

Lucy ponders a moment:

Lucy: *I'm going to my room.*

So be it; would have been lovely to spend the night with her.

Me: *Goodnight, Lucy. It was lovely to spend time with you.*

She kisses me gently on the neck:

Lucy: *Come with me.*

So we end up in her bed for a night of the sort of exercise I've not experienced for some time this side of hot yoga, downward dog an' all.

My lips are sealed at this point; being nominated for a bad sex literary award would be humiliating enough were I writing fiction. It was clear, however, from her enthusiasm that she too had been in the sexual wilderness for some time and came at me with all the confidence and total lack of inhibition that middle age endows us all with as compensation for a body we fear is on the turn.

I spotted that night, for the first but far from the last time, how experience of life sometimes gives women very low expectations of blokes. When I returned to my room in the early hours to take my contact lenses out Lucy didn't expect to ever see me again. Why not? Almost the best bit is sleeping and waking with someone you care about. Not only did I return 10 minutes later but also a few weeks later for a whole weekend of talking, walking and much more of the same.

Was it a one-night stand? No. Not just because we met for that second weekend but also because we'd first met at college. Also and not least a one-night stand pejoratively implies you don't have an emotional connection with the other person. With Lucy I discovered for the first time that sharing stories and showing life's scars creates a bond far greater than the timeline of acquaintance might suggest. That grief, loss and pain can fast-track emotional immersion is a lesson I would never have chosen but one that allows me to say, writing months later, that I have still never had a one-night stand in my life.

As far as the future with Lucy was concerned we concluded that while we got on brilliantly, geographically we were too far apart and given she had a son in his mid-20s, we were also at very different life stages. So we left things there, neither of us regretting anything of the super time we'd spent together.

My only trouble was whether I should tell *Guardian* readers about it in Adam's column. Perhaps not, unless I want to risk alienating people who won't understand the screaming need a bereaved person can have for adult human contact with the opposite sex. Even to just hold and be held skin to skin is enough. This red-hot desire is usually pushed to one side for months, even years, out of proximity to a loved one's death. After my New Year's resolution to seize life, what I had done was acknowledge and embrace that physical fulfilment is a massive part of that story.

Perhaps sharing this adventure with at least 160,000 people, including all those close relatives and friends who know my identity, should have been one to avoid. I didn't duck it, though, even if WAY chum Andy, the only widower I know and who now has a partner and knows about Adam, suggested I do so:

Andy: *Well done, mate! Like you I thought I'd fall apart but absolutely didn't – it was the right time and it was bloody great!*

Me: *Thanks. Look, you know I write "The Widower of the Parish", should I go public about this one?*

Andy: *Do you want a potential shit storm your way?*

Me: *Er…No.*

Andy: *Then don't do it. It took me ages to share the news that I was back making the beast with two backs and frankly it didn't go down too well with Emma's family, friends and practically everyone who found out second hand.*

Me: *How long did it take them to accept it?*

Andy: *I'll let you know…*

Other than thinking that only a teacher would choose that Shakespearian sexual allusion, I didn't embrace his advice at all and submitted the "first sex" copy to *The Guardian*. I did so because:

1. It happened!
2. It was always going to happen sometime.

3. It was not a one-night stand.
4. It couldn't be more hurtful than my admission of falling in love with sister-in-loss Jo months ago and that had been OK (I think).
5. It was joyful rather than miserable for a change.
6. It was a key moment of turnaround on my journey.

The winning argument to myself was no. 7 – would I be happy for Millie and Matt to know about Lucy? The answer was unequivocally a big "yes".

Andy's advice to avoid sharing the Lucy story actually made my decision to publish easier, underlining that my journey is my own and to edit events would mean losing stuff that might bring support, comfort and permission to behave this way to other bereaved folk. Lucie Brownlee's writing about shagging her plumber in *Life After You* made my return to the sexual land of the living so much easier and I hoped to do the same for others – a sort of sexual chain reaction!

On publication, other than a tiny amount of criticism again on Twitter from fellow bereaved with different grief trajectories to my own, which other users largely dealt with, the "Lucy" column seemed not to ruffle feathers or affront plumage in any way.

I had once again through Adam been able to inform well-wishers, friends and relatives in newsprint of my evolution back to the land of the living in a way I could never have done sober, or probably ever, in person. Chalk up yet another unintended positive of being Adam.

As for my behaviour? The Lucy episode did not assuage

the raging libido built up over many months but instead engorged and released it. It was not just sex, though; even more than that I wanted adult female company and companionship, someone to care about and be cared for by; someone maybe to fall in love with. That they might also be terrific in bed was a happy travelling companion to those more emotive needs.

You'd think what could possibly be wrong or go wrong with such a simple ambition?

32.

CLOSING AND OPENING DOORS

My house is packed with portkeys (the portkey is a very simple travelling device in Harry Potter, being an everyday object that has been enchanted to instantly bring anyone who touches it to a specific destination).

Using a portkey is described as like having a hook "somewhere behind the navel" pulling the traveller to their destination. No disrespect intended but the portkeys in my home are so much more powerful than anything from JK Rowling's imagination. Mine can take me not just to another place but to another time.

Simply seeing one of Helen's possessions takes me on a journey back to happier times, places and people. Far from operating behind the navel, they tear at my body and spirit in multiple daily reminders of loss.

The subject of what to do with Helen's belongings has been one on which I've been in receive mode from friends and family for some time:

"Clear everything to help you move on."
"Don't clear too much as you'll regret it later."
"Involve the kids in what to keep."
"Don't inflict clearing their mum's stuff on the kids."
"Do it now".
"Do it next year."
"Don't do it."

So that's all clear, then.

I'm standing in front of a wardrobe full of Helen's clothes. Running my hands over their fabrics and textures is like a download of who she was, her life stages and passions. I love it. I hate it.

I shut the door and shut my mind to it for another week, having dealt already with the random objects of the bedroom – the combs, glasses, makeup etc – and felt better for it, but this is so much. Too much.

Every one of Helen's belongings is an expression of her conscious mind's choices and tastes. Some of them, like her coat and hats, still smell of her and to me are more evocative of Helen than the ashes I'm so studiously avoiding having anything to do with.

I spin the time-turner on my own memories. I'm eight and can picture my mother standing beside a drawer in her bedroom – *"Dad's drawer"*. In it sat those objects which she'd salvaged after his death in 1968.

Mum: *I kept your dad's watch, cufflinks, ring, electric razor and a few other bits and pieces for you, Roger and Richard to cherish when you grow up.*

Later, years later, I was given the cufflinks, Roger the watch and Richard the ring, which was great but I remember so clearly when no one was around, going through the drawer's contents item by item, time after time, year after year.

To me, with so little memory of my dad, he was summed up by his gold jewellery, glasses, handkerchiefs, golf club membership and, rather surprisingly looking back, a membership card for the Playboy Club in swinging 60s London. Racy Daddy!

Would I really want Helen to be summed up like this for the kids in some random objects, ones that might have meant nothing to her and which she might have binned at any time?

No, nor do I ever want to repeat the scene in which having given some of my effortlessly stylish late mother's outfits to charity, I saw one of them walking towards me on the seafront with a different, young face on top. Head-melting stuff.

Pete as per usual provides a counterpoint to my angst:

Pete: *You're over-intellectualising this, matey. Confucius says get some boxes and stick the whole lot in the fucking loft and park it there for a few years. The kids matter, not stuff.*

Bullseye, Pete.

So I order 20 large plastic boxes and it all goes into the loft. This leaves a few big life-affirming positives in play – paintings, photos and ornaments.

No doubt when I die all the boxes of Helen's stuff will

be unpacked by Millie and Matt, hopefully not as testimony to my indecision and Pete's wisdom but as exhibits of their dad's love for their mum that belie the daft, incontinent, grumpy old bastard I'd become.

Having finally got around to doing this, I feel a massive rush of positivity in the simple act of touching Helen's belongings and focusing on the things that she loved and which defined her. It also feels good to be making more decisions to move forward, driving events instead of being driven by them.

So I now have a whole fresh focus in updating and improving the house, starting with the crappy 1950s hardboard doors that Helen had hated and yet we'd never got around to replacing.

On Monday I find myself in the door showroom on a local trading estate. It's only 11am but already it feels like a very long day. Sales specialist Brenda puts down her pen.

Brenda: *OK, that's the doors ordered.*

I pull out my payment card, only for her to glance coldly at it.

Brenda: *Good, now we look at handles!*

She slams another huge catalogue onto the counter between us. The heavy thunk is like an executioner's axe as another hour of my life hits the floor.

Then she pauses, head on shoulder, eyeballing me

in what seems to be an act of door-furniture-induced coquetry.

Brenda: *But first how do you feel about escutcheons?*

My hop into town is now running at two hours and counting. I've looked at endless variations on the woody theme, suffering from the tyranny of far too much choice.

Added to which pain are unwelcome memories prompted by flicking through another high-end door sales brochure. I flashed back several months to sitting with Helen's sister Sarah, studying coffin specifications at the undertaker's. Even the names are similar – Lincoln, Nostalgia, Hamilton, Cleveland, Senator, Westminster – three of these being doors for opening frequently and three having lids for closing only once. Do manufacturers think these names help? It says something about my new mindset that I now shrug, not shudder, at emotional ambushes like this; even chuckling at the absurdity.

I noticed that more of my memories of Helen were now of the 24 years before she was ill, which armours me with a much stronger buffer against grief's sharpest onslaughts. If she would have laughed, then so now do I – and she laughed a lot.

Writing this, I would suggest "laugh like your lover" is a great action standard for the bereaved spouse to seek new humour and happiness. Assuming the spouse in question was not a misery guts!

What I don't have is a buffer against Brenda's well-intentioned but bottomless enthusiasm for her job. I'm

Alan Rickman's character in *Love Actually*, whose quick exit from the jewellery counter is thwarted by Rowan Atkinson's overzealous Christmas-wrapping routine.

I'm afraid to open my mouth in case it adds another layer of complexity and delay. And what the buggery bollocks is an escutcheon anyway?

Much, much later, as payment goes through, Brenda looks up from the card machine, takes off her glasses and skewers me with a Paddington Bear-scale hard stare.

Brenda: *Will they be well hung or are you going to upset me by doing it yourself?*

I stare back, not sensing any mirth at these Carry On-like double entendres, as she continues:

Brenda: *I can't bear it when people go DIY and come back because they have cocked up.*

My stifled snigger is overwhelmed by the implied insult to my hunter-gatherer DIY prowess. I am very good at DIY; not because I prowl the house in a tool belt but because I know what elements I do well and leave to professionals those jobs I'm profoundly crap at.

I reassure Brenda with:

Me: *Don't worry, I've a man who'll hang them for me.*

She looks happy.

Brenda: *Great. I'd prefer to sell fewer doors than have blokes cock up when they're not well hung.*

Still not a flicker of humour or irony passes her face. Is this her game of is it mine? I take my receipt and make a swift exit while it's still daylight and before Sid James appears lewdly from stage left.

I do have a man in fact, albeit an old one. The brilliant, semi-retired chippy Frank, who is currently painting the house with barely a wry smile at my "feature wall" colour plan he is meant to be following. Brilliantly good value, he can hang three doors in six hours.

I think that sorting Helen's belongings has spawned an urge to nest in me perhaps comparable to that experienced by some women in the third trimester of pregnancy – maybe grief and death have trimesters like birth and life.

33.

MAKING MEMORIES

"It's like you're Jason Bourne, only older and not so buff!" shrieks Jeannie as we sit comparing notes and news on our loss.

She's a friend, met through WAY (Widowed & Young) whose partner died at a similar time to Helen and we've swapped stories in person and online for months.

Her mocking response to my offloading to her would seem disrespectful from anyone other than a fellow grief traveller. However, Jeannie's back-story is even harder than mine: her husband's death was sudden and self-inflicted. So we laugh, comrades in adversity sharing memories and most definitely just friends.

We'd been talking about grief taboos and, of course, the subject of sex fuels the laughter of our conversation as I'd been wondering whether there would be any late comeback now that the Lucy column had been published:

Jeannie: *So you, a middle-aged single man, has sex with a single woman of similar age; what's the big deal?*

Bloody well done, you!

She raises her glass, downing her wine a little too quickly as she did the last and the two before that. I sense in her the same easy enjoyment of alcohol that I had fallen into. Hopefully it is a necessary part of her upward rebuild and not oiling a downward slope.

Me: *Try adding the word "widowed" before "man". Then stick "within 12 months of his wife dying'" to the end of your sentence and you invite the jury in!*

Jeannie shrugs and drunk or not wisely pushes it back at me:

Jeannie: *And has their verdict been a problem?*

Actually, people have been really supportive. Yes, my mate Pete and cousin Holly feign surprise that any woman would want to shag me, but they are cheerleaders for the fact that Lucy plugged a hole in my sensual wellbeing and recovery.

I've called it wrong in fearing a backlash once again. The whole sex-in-bereavement piece seems less a taboo than I'd imagined even if it's a gig never spoken of or even acknowledged.

Having put the subject of Lucy to bed, Jeannie and I move on to what has become for me a taboo of a very personal kind – the fact that despite being married to Helen for 19 years and being together for seven before that, I somehow have no real memory of us living together.

Of course I remember Helen; in fact the good news is as time passes since she died, so thin and unwell, I increasingly recall her as she was before her fucking cancer, which is a fabulous development. But the whole nature of domestic cohabitation, joint decision making, constructive compromises, even sharing a bed every night and waking every morning with her, feels vague and almost absent.

When I say this out loud, anyone listening goes into shock. Even my brilliant and deadpan counsellor, Heidi, made one of her breathy noises when I told her. Jeannie's eyes open wide also in what I assumed was the same reaction but wasn't.

Jeannie: *That's exactly how I feel! Dave and I were together for years, but now when I imagine living with him, there's no sense of ever having done so.*

Snap! This care and connectivity is what WAY is about.

Prodded unremittingly but gently by Heidi in our last consultation, I'd unpacked this grief amnesia:

Me: *It's like when Helen died my memory banks were largely erased. Everything has pretty much gone and what's left is now filtered through grief and disruption.*
Heidi: *Meaning?*
Me: *I need to rebuild for the future. I need to make sense of why some of the past has just gone!*

Sitting now drinking too much with Jeannie, her film analogy is not as mad as I sound reporting all this. It is Bourne-like! As if I'd suddenly woken up with the kids, family, friends, a home, a job and am looking for clues about what I feel about them, who I am now and how to do the best I can in making the right calls to bring up Millie and Matt, manage relationships, work, love, sex, the future. Everything.

Like Bourne sitting in the diner not knowing why he instinctively notices registrations on cars in the parking lot, I find myself instinctively judging whether everything that crosses my path has value for my new life or not and then acting on this new input.

This extends to people, work, possessions, and even, it seems, my own memories, in which I've wiped stuff that doesn't help me deal with the present. Looking back, it's part of the reason why I changed so much in the months since Helen died, needing as I did new content to replace that lost.

My comfort is that despite having jettisoned so much of my recall of our lives together, my love of Helen is sharper and stronger than ever. I remember the purple and scarlet times, not the beige ones, however much I'd do anything to have them back. Heidi as ever had shone her light in the direction I needed to go to see this for myself without spelling it out too much:

Heidi: *Maybe the memories you've lost were the ones that don't matter and make the ones you keep matter more.*

It is true. Helen and I are conjoined closer by my remaining uncluttered memories of the high point of our past even as we are separated by the future.

Good for me, maybe, but it makes me more fearful than before about the kids and their memories of their mum. If my own have been so reworked by grief with all my 26 years of history to construct positive recollections, what about Millie and Matt, whose conscious, non-baby time with Helen was so cruelly short? How will they remember the best of her when they have so much less material to work with that is free of her decline and death?

The answer, or at least a good crack at an answer, has an unlikely conception as I sit in the sort of northern pub I thought only existed in old newsreels or reruns of *Get Carter*. It still has a throwback to that era in the form of a small stage, in the corner of which under a low-wattage spotlight performs probably the worst singer in this or any world.

It's not even karaoke night, but a paid performance as Stella, of "Starlit Stella" billing, belts out "The Way We Were" in a manner that massacres Barbra Streisand's signature song, rewriting it with a six-inch paintbrush. The lyrics to this mega hit are often transcribed for professionals with the opening word as "Mem'ries". Stella favours, instead, the full nine syllables "Meeeemoreeeyaa aayyeeaahyeeeaaaeeess".

Yet I remain grateful for her brassy enthusiasm. She's pounded the word not only into the corners but also the front, centre, ceiling and dado rails of my mind. There it sits on the long drive south, stirring and provoking the whole issue of how memories are provoked and preserved.

I feel at last that, thanks to the passage of time, I am robust enough to think about Helen in a way that accepts she has gone but that her love and legacy for us all is preserved. My certainty that I can now do this is reflected in the fact I have many fewer grief ambushes where unexpected reminders of Helen's death cloak me in darkness.

How now to further seed and propagate Helen's memory for Millie and Matt, just as they evoke her simply by existing for me? I see in their faces flashes of us both – a successful fusing of features that caused me to say to Helen in an outburst she never let me forget, what became a running joke as to my unthinking honesty:

Me: *How did we have such beautiful children?*
Helen: *Sorry?*
Me: *The kids, how come they are so beautiful given we...*
Helen: *Yes? Given we what?*
Me (silence): ...
Helen (looking outraged): *Go on...*
Me: *Nothing. Absolutely nothing.*

Helen's pretence at anger broke as she roared with laughter:

Helen: *You mean how did we have children who are so much more beautiful than we are? Maybe ask the milk-man!*
Me (relieved and grinning): *It's a milk-woman!*
Helen (snorting with mirth): *The mystery deepens.*

Recalling this brings to mind a quote from schooldays struggling over A level Latin, *"Memory is the treasury and guardian of all things,"* so says Cicero. Better perhaps, *"It's the laughter we will remember, whenever we remember the way we were"* – so sings Stella, badly, but accurately.

It's true, though, that the kids' resemblance to Helen is more than enough that they are and will be for me cherished three-dimensional daily reminders of my truly beautiful wife.

By contrast, I feel that Millie and Matt are growing up and away from who they were when she died, that I need to create and curate positive reminders of Helen to keep her with them as their lives expand.

Doing so may also break the barrier in their minds formed by images of the emaciated, ill, barely conscious Helen in the final 48 hours of her life. This image of impending death sits golem-like between them and their recalling her as their beautiful, happy, living and loving mum. This insight is not me being smart, but the kids being honest as Millie tells me with a tragic matter-of-factness:

Millie: *Every time I think of Mum, it's the last time I saw her lying so ill in the hospital bed before she died. She barely knew us.*

This sucks. I want them to think of Helen as validation of the vibrancy of their own lives – not as a symbol of death and fragility. Screw memento mori, embrace memento vivere ("remember to live" if your Latin is rusty).

So we have the two "we love Mum" projects.

Her simple and beautifully illustrated Inspector Hound stories we're having designed with a view to publishing ourselves or finding a publisher (www.inspectorhound.co.uk). It's a family project simmering happily along over many months; an active memorial for the kids so that Helen will not be time-locked in history, left behind just because her own clock stopped.

He was one of the characters we'd briefed to stained-glass artist Tony for our second project, the five memorial stained-glass panels for the house. The selection of the images and the anticipation and update on their progress are as valuable to the kids as the panels themselves. Once installed and backlit by the sun, they will be constant, dynamic reminders of Helen, there for us every day and overlooking the lives in which she is not present, but is still part of.

I am really passionate about these stained-glass home memorials and stained-glass art in general. My note to Tony drafted when I was so inspired by dying fellow student Dawn and sent only when my job was ending, has received a reply. Fabulously, he's readily agreed to take me on as his trainee.

In time, I hope to paint windows for others who want a memorial that doesn't involve a cemetery trip, photo album or laptop. When writing all this up for Adam's column I'd thought to myself that the whole idea of the memorial windows was a good one but was I too close to it? As someone who had worked in marketing and done much research, I couldn't resist the idea of crowdsourcing the knowledge and judgment of *Guardian* readers. So against my better instinct for secrecy, I published Adam's e-mail address asking for advice.

I'm so glad I did, as there were almost immediately and constantly since, a rush then a trickle of views, all positive and massively helpful. My momentum to do something with this stained-glass idea is now buoyed by hundreds of smart people's validation that I am not deluded by grief-driven wishful thinking.

I'd asked also for ideas on the name for the memorial windows. To this there was an unexpected and consistent response:

> *Memorial Windows says what they are but it's a gloomy name. Memorials are made of stone or granite, and things of darkness set in graveyards. Your idea is about lighting a life at home.*

This consistent line of logic gave rise to many name suggestions, with a consistent theme that the windows should be called "Lifelights" – windows on lives well lived and loved.

I remain grateful to everyone for their help and to the column for easing me further along my journey once again. Lifelights ahoy. (www.golightlyglass.com)

34.

Dipping into Dating

And still the wave of my New Year's positivity refuses to break, surging me forward without too much thought or pause. Not only am I looking after myself better by exercising more and drinking less, I've actually started my stained-glass training and have jumped hook, line and libido into the shark tank of online dating.

I'd discussed which site I should sign up on with settled widower mate Andy:

Me: *I don't think I should date a widow – we're likely to have the whole death thing hanging over us as we hunt for something else in common.*

Andy: *Fair instinct.*

Me: *But I've been wrong before – indeed often am. Maybe seeing someone bereaved who "gets it" would make it all easier. You and I get on.*

Andy: *I don't fancy you and you don't want to go out with me. Seriously maybe don't avoid widows but avoid widower sites as demographics mean the women on there* *will be much older than you – I mean 70 plus . If you don't want a candlelit dinner delivered by meals on wheels don't go there.*

Me: *Did you?*

Andy (wincing): *Like night of the living dead.*

Me: *That's so unkind!*

Andy: *I was kind to them. I'm not sparing you the rough and wrinkles, though, 'cos you're a mate. Don't go there.*

Me: *OK, I get it but I can put in an age range, can't I?*

Andy: *Sure, but do that and then add a 10-mile distance filter and you'll probably only get matched to two women, one of whom may never stop crying and the other hasn't left the house since 1990.*

He's being cruel to be kind and unlike Pete, who would no doubt be just as blunt, Andy has actually lost and looked again for love.

So I duck widow dating sites and the more obvious shag-happy ones. I remember all too well months ago a scene in a lovely hotel on the north-east coast. They were six single women aged 35 to mid-60s – variations on divorced, separated, single, widowed. They met each month to go down and swim in the freezing sea before heading up to the relatively boiling bar. It was very life-affirming and their mood intoxicating in itself.

I'd been the only other person drinking there and they'd kindly called me over and enveloped me with their wine and wisdom. They were sympathetic and supportive of my widowerhood but also raucously encouraging of what I should do to return to the land of the "living libido". They all had quite broad north-east accents which I'll try and capture as it adds texture to what was a memorable evening. We'd discussed Tinder:

Single 1: *Man, it's great if yer just wanna get off with someone like.*
Single 2: *Aye. I've used it lots and it's marvellous. Nee strings unless their gonna tie ye to the bed!*

Much laughter.

Single 3: *Mind yer, there can be some straaaange blowks who dinnat get oot much.*
Single 2: *Or like Dave, who said he was a single then I see the rat with his missus at the fair. She knew nowt about his dating.*
Single 4: *Till you telt her.*
Single 3: *Aye. Like a cornered rat. Thought she was gonna push him under a dodgem.*

Much more laughter.

Single 5: *Or like that nice Kevin lad I saw last week. Mind you he smelt.*
Single 6 (resting hand on my knee): *So gan' on one of them sites, bonnie lad, an' you can get yerself back on track an' back in bed!*

There was so much laughter until we all wobbled off on our separate ways; it was gentle, kind-hearted but terrifying stuff. It was and is still extraordinary to me that they all had chosen Tinder in an open-eyed, unreserved way to give them what they wanted, maybe needed. I salute you, nice scary ladies, for your help and extreme honesty.

This really made me think hard about what I was looking for. I chose in the end a much more mainstream site that would get me back on the dating bus, with love as a possible terminus but with many a chance to have some fun riding en route or jump off at the nearest stop if the direction was wrong.

So I edge my way forward from idly searching to writing a profile and uploading the least gargoyle-like photos I can find. I try and configure it as honestly as possible, using recent shots and outlining my dating aspirations, if not all my personal history. Rightly or wrongly, I don't include any reference to my being a widower, preferring to define it in person than have it define me at a distance.

I post it up and I am hit almost immediately by what seems like a torrent of smiling faces and accomplished minds. This is all so fast – how the bloody hell do I filter them?

Without much thought I do what I'd do if I'd met them socially, simply asking myself if I found them attractive. It's a little superficial but at least knocks a few out – and yet it still leaves me a pretty long shortlist. I need help.

I've no fear of sharing all this with the kids so enlist Millie's assistance to work through the profiles. I've printed them out, thanks to a tip from one of the Geordie women, to avoid being seen to click on anyone too often. I'm laughing at myself in hindsight at this attempt not to seem too keen or needy, given where this would lead. Millie I and sit on the bed together with this huge pile of stapled pages like a couple of hungry, happy house hunters who've turned to trading flesh.

Millie brandishes one in a wavy hand.

Millie: *Dad, this one's way too nice for you!*
Me: *Too nice. Blimey, how can you tell?*
Millie: *Look at what she does and how she looks for goodness' sake!*
Me: *You are very rude...*
Millie: *...but right!*

Sure enough, among that morning's lexicon of aspiring love are many women who not only look lovely but also have jobs, interests and passions that set the benchmark high for a bloke whose idea of a good night in post-bereavement now involves greasing his car's suspension (not a metaphor).

I read of delightful women whose "musical" means near-concert-class pianist vs. my torturing Harry the cat with my saxophone.

Then there are others whose lifetime of working for charities contrasts with my own servitude to mammon and, of course, those whose "me on the beach" photo suggests a body toned and trimmed by Pilates, not, as mine, by poppadums.

I wonder whether I'm ready for all this. The clay of my new persona is barely formed and unfired by time and experience. Will it shatter looking for love? I've told no one other than my children and my Widowed & Young mate Andy.

I wonder also whether writing Adam's column will be a problem. Do I keep it quiet or would that be dishonest and would coming clean upfront mean that I'd be exposing my true identity to a date that might end badly and she'd blab? Would anyone but me care?

Posting my profile live online had been an easy, logical step. In the physical world I'd have to socialise for Britain to match the number of single women who cross my screen daily. I could always, I tell myself, cancel it before things got underway or out of hand.

Andy warns me this is naive:

Andy: *Dating online is like getting your house valued then suddenly the estate agent's board's up, a sale's agreed and the removal van packed. It's a conveyor belt laced with dating catnip – once on, you're hooked, mate. Hooked!*

I am hooked but also worried. Living with the decision not to tell my back-story feels wrong, dishonest even. That said, declaring my status may be a big downer – people assuming I'm permanently miserable. But I can't bring myself to easily lie – I'm on emotionally thin ice anyway so I amend my key paragraphs to include statements that allude to a "love of life undiminished by big challenges in recent times" and so, like MP Alan Clark, am "economical with the *actualité*".

Andy had been more blunt – he is, for want of a better

phrase, not only a teacher but a geezer:

Andy: *Say you're a widower and you'll attract women who want to be your bestie not your bird, or death geeks who want a cry-a-long.*

I think now he was wrong. Being coy about the truth was destined to cause issues as women on these sites assumed divorce not death in my history. I should have been more open, relationships which work flourish on full not half truths.

As days pass and the profiles keep pouring in, I realise I've no idea what I'm really looking for. Actually not true, what I really want is to go back to the life I had before Helen was ill. I can't, so mustn't try to recreate the past with an ersatz Helen – what chance of success for anyone cast in that role?

Even making comparisons now to Helen opens up the midlifer's dating challenge that I have already fallen foul of – you end up extrapolating from the tiniest evidence a version of a whole future together – like trying to work out whether you'll love a house from being told it has a phone point in the hall.

I try instead to think of my new screen chums as random fun folk, some of whom I'm very drawn to, as I would be if I met them socially but with the added attraction of knowing they are actually in-market (ugh that phrase), looking to meet someone. The downside of this, in an era of online shopping, is summed up by Millie when I complain there are too many matches:

Millie: *Go on, Dad, put more filters in to make sure you get what you order.*

Her digital native's assumption that you can serve up a relationship like a New Look frock is tempting but flawed – you can't fancy someone more because they live five miles away and chemistry can't be barcoded. So I'm adding visceral to virtual by *smiling* only at the very few women who feel special, irrespective of pretty much any factor other than *non-smoker.*

However, despite trying to relegate online dating to a tea-dance chance to meet some fun, interesting people, Yeats' small voice will still be whispering in the ear of any women I meet:

I have spread my dreams under your feet;
Tread softly because you tread on my dreams.

No pressure or hidden trapdoor then for any girl who agrees to step off the page and meet me. Prophetic words that should have provided more warning.

35.

BOOZE FOR MY BABY?

After so much dating debating, it was almost but not actually a welcome distraction when a few days later Millie tested my single parenting powers as never before.

It had started innocently enough after a gentle evening of "dads' beers". It is said that friends bring happiness into your life but best friends bring beer. It's blokey nonsense, of course, but beer has been good to me, lending a friendly foaming cohesion to the middle-aged school dads who for 10 years I've met monthly for a few Friday night cheeky ones. In recent months "dads' beers" has provided comfort and stability amid the turmoil of Helen's death in a way I could never have guessed and no book would suggest.

Tonight, I'm home a bit later and merrier than intended as we'd swapped the plan to eat out for more time drinking and talking bollocks in the bar. I'm creeping noisily through the front door with exaggerated attempts to be quiet which are anything but quiet. Millie has reached an age when I can go out locally and has been looking after a soundly sleeping Matt. I stick my head round the lounge door and whisper in the not very *sotto voce* of the mildly inebriated:

Me: *Hello? Millie, are you awake?*

She appears silently behind me (how do women do this?), her head resting on her shoulder, appraising me with a look of warm indulgence that makes her seem older than her years. With what she must have thought was pitch-perfect timing, given I've had a few and am feeling guilty about being out late, she asks:

Millie: *Dad, will you buy me some alcohol for Michelle's party?*
Me: *What?*
Millie: *Maybe Bacardi Breezers and a bottle of Jack Daniels.*

She's overplayed her hand. Her libertine and fair father when half-cut is more, not less, likely to be immediately substituted by Victorian despot dad:

Me: *No way! Go to bed. Go to bed now. Love you.*
Millie: *But… but…*
Me (shouting): *Not interested. Now!*

So it has happened. A tough teenage question with a binary right/wrong answer to which I've no clue.

The advertising executive David Ogilvy was still connected to his business when I worked there as a graduate. I particularly liked and still do like his maxim:

Ogilvy: *Fight for your Queens; let the Pawns go.*

This has been my mantra over many years but particularly since Helen died. I seek to run an easygoing ship but one where the boundaries of the deck are well understood and ultimately I remain the captain even if mainly in my own eyes.

Millie's question is obviously an Ogilvy "Queen". Too harsh a response and I sow the seeds of rebellion and mutiny; too lax and I am on a course to blow my commitment to Helen not to screw up the kids by crappy solo parenting – not how I expressed it when holding her hand in her final hours but pretty close.

The next day in the cold and certainly sober light of a Saturday morning I have much remorse at the state of my headache and how harshly I'd denied her request for small amounts of booze while being on the outside of rather too much of it myself. Unfairly, Millie's reward for her babysitting had been my shouting at her request for a quite modest and honest two Bacardi Breezers and what turned out to be a Jack Daniels *miniature*.

At her age I was buying cans of Kestrel and vodka and drinking them with friends in parks. Being at boarding school, the issue of parental consent or discussion never featured but would I have talked to my mum or indeed anyone as openly as Millie is talking to me? Probably not; my OTT reaction had been wrong at every level – bad dad.

My more considered view has much less of a problem with her desire to release her booze genie from its bottle(s).

What to do? It is exactly the sort of dilemma Helen would know how to handle and I miss so much her good sense and rock-solid value set. I'm likely to get it wrong. As I have become so much better at doing without grief, I imagine a short conversation with Helen – I can't be the only widower/widow who does this surely?

Me: *There's a right answer to Millie but I've no idea what it is.*

Helen: *What did your mum say to you at Millie's age? She was a single parent.*

Me: *Nothing at all.*

Helen: *Did she let you drink?*

Me: *Actually, yes. Beer and lager, wine with meals even before that.*

Helen: *And did you abuse it?*

Me: *No. There was no need to – it was always available and my mum knew.*

Helen: *What about spirits?*

Me: *No. I never dared ask. Children don't ask their parents that sort of thing.*

Helen: *And yet …*

Me: *…Millie is asking me, which is a good thing.*

Helen: *De-dah! Prize to the man with the sore head.*

She was right even as a voice embedded in my soul.

I guess I should be thankful, and perhaps my pleasure at Millie's smart honesty left a permissive door open, which she now shoulders through as we talk over breakfast:

Millie: *Dad, you went to parties at my age – was there alcohol?*

Me (guardedly; there's going to be a catch): *Some.*

Millie: *So you'll see, Dad, if I don't have my own alcohol I'll end up sipping lots of other people's, which is worse.*

Me: *Worse for whom and in what way?*

Millie: *Worse for me than if I had my own. If you buy me alcohol I'll know exactly what I'm drinking and so end up drinking less.*

It's a great argument, offering me control at a distance, assuming I take her at her word. I'm going to say "yes" but am still tempted to take counsel from other parents in case I'm the only parent who buys booze. The fact that in the event I don't take advice, other than from Helen, is because I'm loath to be seen as not coping by asking for help. Also, in this more sensitive instance I worry that if I take advice and then ignore it I'll be causing unnecessary offence.

So I treat the problem like a work project and do some fieldwork by buying double the amount of booze she's requested and drinking it in less than an hour, partially through a straw, as they've been known to do. It's not going to get her vulnerably drunk.

This takes place in full view of Millie because I don't want any growing up rite-of-passage to intrude on the brilliant honesty of our relationship since Helen died. I know that most parents tell themselves that their children are open with them and are often at some point proven dramatically wrong. But with the three of us I believe this to be totally and tragically true. Millie and Matt know that no conversation we would ever have can be worse than the one that began *"Your mum is so very ill she's likely to die tomorrow".* Certainly no conversation about booze, boyfriends, money or gynaecological problems will or should ever get near, please God.

So I buy the booze and am clearly not the only parent to do so. She and her super-heavily made-up squad head off to the party looking fabulous and innocent despite their merrily clinking bags.

It works. Later it's clear Millie is tiddly but not drunk and one or two friends who have sourced their own booze or sipped from others' bottles, including neat vodka, are in a much worse state, having discovered that long hair and being sick in the garden is a tricky combination. One is silent in the back of my car, which has me on edge that she is about to park a custard on my leather, another talks incessantly, albeit not in a language anyone might recognise as English or possibly human.

I've made the right call, so hurrah for me. It's a good feeling and I'm a bit smug about it. It's annoying, therefore, when I hear there's parental misinformation as to the size of the whisky bottle Millie was packing:

Parent: *I can't believe Millie's dad let her take a whole bottle of Jack Daniels to Michelle's party!*

So up a long ladder of teenage trust and down a small gossipy snake which, like a few cheeky dads' beers, I'm happy to stomach.

36.

NAVIGATING GRIEFBERGS

From the day I started running marathons I made every mistake possible – started too fast, too slow, trained too little, too much, drank too little, tripped up and over a nice man dressed as an already endangered white rhino and in a low point was overtaken by a bloke dressed as a tub of Utterly Butterly. This may prove a parallel experience as even now, right at the beginning of my passage through online dating, I sense I will end up tracking pretty much every high and low that this truly addictive way of meeting people may offer. Prophetically perhaps I believe being a widower adds an extra tight bend in what is already a crazily difficult course to navigate.

This is a big bleak assumption for me to extrapolate from only one date, "Nicky from Cambridge", but I have already broken the biggest rule of this new sport. I'd spent a few weeks e-mailing her from the dating site, a fact which according to former *Guardian* columnist Stella Grey's *Midlife Ex-Wife* online dating tips, is usually the kiss of death. Stella was right in that not only was there a complete lack of chemistry but we seemed to have nothing left to say over lunch that we hadn't already written. This was probably a facet of the chemistry bypass but wasn't helped by the fact that her profile photos were clearly many years old, an inherent dishonesty that matters in the micrometre-sensitive, sliding-doors world of online dating and probably made my glass attitudinally half-empty from the outset.

Despite this, I remain more than half in love with the sheer excitement of it all, which has led me to tonight's date with Monica. Sitting in a pretty upmarket London restaurant, I gaze across the dining table into Monica's dark, slightly beady eyes. This is harder than it sounds as I am trying manfully to ignore the large hungry-looking vulture perched on her shoulder as they both pick over Helen's life and, more horribly, her death.

I dramatise for effect but anyone who's read the *His Dark Materials* trilogy will understand Philip Pullman's clever creation was to give characters "dæmons" which would often sit on their shoulders. These were physical manifestations of their inner selves in the form of a specific animal, fixed in adulthood but subject to change in children.

Monica's was definitely a vulture. Taller than me, thin, brilliantly made up with sharply ridged cheek bones and unusually, almost black eyes, her beauty is fast fading under my disillusioned gaze. She's increasingly resembling her mangy, thin-faced, feathered friend. Both flutter excitedly as she pokes her beak harder into the corpse of Helen's history.

Monica: *So how long did your poor wife battle against the big C before she died?*

I'd already explained in advance by e-mail my back-story and Helen's death; all responses to some quite personal but seemingly innocent questions. But Monica's vulture, I see in hindsight, was already hatched in these prying e-mails; a warm-up for the white-hot heat of this first-date inquisition. We are barely into our mains; fittingly, hers is sirloin served almost rare. My initial upset at her ghoulish interest is becoming a surging wave of anger, swollen by the figurative use of "battle" and "big C", both terms hated by Helen and so by me also.

Monica: *So did your wife suffer much or was it quick at the end?*

The wave breaks over me and just for a moment I want to hurt her. Without Heidi's help after the near miss of the car park punch-up, I might have face-planted her peaky features into her bloody dinner. Instead, and for the very first time ever, I stand up and slightly theatrically toss tenners onto the table and walk out of the restaurant.

I shouldn't have looked back but do and get to see her flapping her wings in surprise, then shrugging to other diners or perhaps a non-existent studio audience to invoke sympathy at my bad behaviour. No doubt, baldy bird hidden safely from sight, she will squawk to friends later:

Monica: *Never ever date a widower – they're emotionally unstable and rude with it!*

Later I delete her profile – the words "scavenging", "crass" and "voyeuristic" somehow missing from it. This has knocked me back. It was my second date and a negative build on the chemistry-free first one with "old photos" Nicky.

I hope that I carry few prejudices or preconceptions. I am aware I am running in there arms open, looking for love and happiness with all its emotional and physical intimacy but hope that doesn't show so obviously as to make me look needy. Beyond that, there had been no assumptions, despite my friend Pete's jibes:

Pete: *He wants a date to live next door, have retired recently as a swimsuit model, their dad to own a brewery and a PhD in astrophysics.*

The fact that a friend can josh me about this suggests I have come a long way and can push back in the same vein and joke:

Me: *Wrong as usual, my friend: she could have any science-based doctorate.*

A lifetime alone beckons ever closer…

I shouldn't let Monica's nastiness stop me but that meeting misfire left a bad taste and I found it emotionally damaging and draining. It all feels like Russian roulette but one in which I've only pulled the trigger twice and both times found bullets tearing into me. I still wonder how overt I should be about the fact and recency of Helen dying, given people's dubious ability to process that fact. We all carry baggage at this life stage but mine seems less common on what is not a specialist widow/widower site.

Knowing I've Helen's blessing to be out there counts for so much and means I have no guilt, hang-ups or desire to find a carbon copy of her. Maybe that thought is missing from my profile. It might remove unseen obstacles and make for better dates or at least help avoid further misfires. Maybe I should have asked Helen to help write it as per author Amy Krouse Rosenthal's heartbreakingly beautiful *New York Times* letter looking for a new partner for her husband, even as she lay dying.

Revisiting it now, it is again the final paragraph that sucks the air out of the room for me:

> *I am wrapping this up on Valentine's Day, and the most genuine, non-vase-oriented gift I can hope for is that the right person reads this, finds Jason, and another love story begins. I'll leave this intentional empty space below as a way of giving you two the fresh start you deserve.*

I don't know Jason but whatever the beauty of his wife's writing I am pretty sure that for him Valentine's Day is anything but an empty space given their years together.

As for me, surveying the usually calm waters of my desk diary, I see several difficult days poking through. These emotional pinnacles have hidden pathos capable of ripping holes in the side of the good ship positivity that had endured since Christmas and New Year.

Unlike the *Titanic*'s hapless lookouts, I can see at a distance grief's peaks and can at least plan around them. I'd told counsellor Heidi that although ostensibly the most difficult day is the anniversary of Helen dying, I fear it the least:

Me: *It's just a date and one that I see no reason to mark. It's not even the worst day, such was the inevitability of death by then.*

That accolade belongs to a day a few days earlier when I was ushered into a side room by a nurse:

Nurse: *You do understand what's happening here? Helen is going to die in the next few hours or days.*

So burst the bubble of hope that Helen might pull out of her downward spiral. It had prompted the truly worst conversation a few hours later when I had to tell Millie and Matt that their mum was dying and so smother Matt's belief there was a chance of her recovery:

Matt: *There's always hope, Dad.*
Me: *No there isn't, darling.*

Worst day. Best forgotten.

Helen's birthday by comparison is impossible to ignore, so I plan to embrace it by planting in the garden a tree whose blossom will in time mark the passing of the seasons, replacing short-term grief at her death with long-term memories of her life. I'd already spoken to the sympathetic nursery, which would make every effort to make special the kids' selection of a sapling.

For them, the date to hate may be bleeding Mothering Sunday, which rises up like a tombstone with all its weeks of high-street build-up. I'm going to embrace *keeping friends close and enemies closer* by this and every Mother's Day re-enthusing the kids about their mother's favourite things and sharing photos and memories of her. I hope they'll see afresh Helen's passions and personality.

The day of dread for the worst of times is for me Valentine's Day, the very one Amy Krouse Rosenthal welcomed as a gateway to the future.

Helen and I hadn't paid too much attention to its cheesy celebration of a love that should matter as much the other 364 days. I think this was why we both liked the song "My Funny Valentine" with its last line speaking no lies, "Every day is Valentine's Day", especially as sung somewhat surprisingly by Matt Damon in *The Talented Mr Ripley*.

Valentine's Day for this year and every year will carry embedded images of our last together.

In the early days following her diagnosis, Helen and I, in an unspoken attempt to populate her remaining time with beautiful memories, had paid a visit to Simon Rogan's L'Enclume in beautiful Cartmel. We'd been inspired by seeing Rob Brydon and Steve Coogan plough and play their way through the lunch menu on the BBC's *The Trip*.

Travelling at Helen's insistence by train to help us take it all in and relax, we'd stopped at Carnforth where *Brief Encounter* was filmed and had tea in the Refreshment Room recreated there.

It was in tribute to that happy trip weeks before that she'd booked to watch the film at our favourite cinema on Valentine's Day, not thinking that by then she would have been in hospital a week, with husband and then children having been given "the talk" about her impending passing.

But fate, fucking cancer, her consultant and I had not reckoned on Helen's love of life, as she lay there so very ill, drips dangling and life ebbing:

Helen: *I will go to the cinema tonight. I absolutely will.*

We'd all been sceptical but go we did, against advice and in a "borrowed" wheelchair to sit at one of the cabaret tables, which the lovely old art deco cinema offered me with much kindness on hearing of the situation.

There we'd drunk gin, eaten cheese and watched Trevor Howard and Celia Johnson lost in love but separated by circumstance.

Looking back, I'd seen in the eyes of the people who had moved over to let us through to our seats both shock and compassion at Helen's clearly emaciated and dying state but it didn't dent the moment, indeed it has somehow inscribed the memory.

Next 14 February, like every one, I'll seize the day as

Helen seized every day and spend time at her memorial, knowing with certainty the truth in Carol Ann Duffy's words carved so beautifully into the Welsh slate and repeated in the opening of this book.

So while I love the honesty of Amy Krouse Rosenthal's letter and I know that Helen would understand and share its sentiment, I could not easily believe in its assumption that being out their dating is being on the road to finding new true love. Indeed, the very mention of Valentine's Day and a delayed emotional backlash from my recent Monica moment of rage and upset had made flaccid my commitment to be out there at all. So, discouraged, I returned to my profile and rewrote the opening paragraph to announce in the least needy statement ever:

> *I have decided already that online dating is not for me now, maybe not for me forever. Good luck to the lovely people I am sure are out there.*

And then I, or rather Adam, had a call from the BBC asking me to take part in a radio programme with Amy Krouse Rosenthal's letter as a discussion point for a group of bereaved people in the US and UK.

I was happy to agree and on the day it was with childlike wonder at being on the radio that I heard myself introduced:

Host: *We're speaking to Adam Golightly, who writes for* The Guardian *about the loss of his wife and his attempts to rebuild his life and seek new love.*

This certainly sounds better than what I might have written:

Not the Host: *We're speaking to Adam Golightly, who despite the calmness of his column is a jobless, emotional train wreck; driven by emotion and erection, this clueless loser is blundering into online dating certain to find misadventure.*

Just sayin'.

However the panel was really positive and articulate. We all got on well, with the experience of loss creating instant connections across distance and differing demographics. I was a little disingenuous in that after sharing some of my own story I also shared my stated enthusiasm for dating, which at the time, thanks to Valentine's Day and Monica, had pretty much gone.

Me: *I'm out there because I've a massive capacity for love and don't accept that the rest of my life has to be unhappy, it's not what Helen wanted or what my children need. It doesn't in any way mean I love or loved Helen any less but love IS different without her here.*

What was great was that all the other bereaved people were fabulously supportive and there was a lot of *"I know just how Adam feels"*, which was ironic since I was so unsure myself. Surprisingly and wonderfully, listening to the programme again afterwards, I felt as if a weight had been lifted. Hearing my words played back and being accepted and applauded by other bereaved respondents was remarkably positive and somehow gave me greater certainty that I was doing OK, even by dating.

So I went back online to discover that, far from putting women off, my declaration that I was quitting had provoked more "smiles" and messages of enquiry than ever before. Human nature is odd and there is nothing so attractive as what is no longer available, it seems. Out of mischief and career-long instinct not to change something that successfully sells, I left it up – not having asked Helen to write me my own Amy Krouse Rosenthal style of profile, I need every advantage I can get.

With the shameful wisdom of hindsight I should probably have added:

> As well as having a very large Siberian Forest cat, his bereavement makes him possibly the worst boyfriend material in the world.

This may not have turned out to be any less compelling, perhaps, but would probably have been more honest.

36.

CALL ME CARACTACUS

Most dating profiles don't require you to give your full name but if they did I'd write:

Me: *The name is Potts, Caractacus Potts.*

It might just be! You will understand the reason for my Bond-like delivery if you know that the film *Chitty Chitty Bang Bang* was based on the children's book by Bond author Ian Fleming and produced by Bond supremo Cubby Broccoli.

Unsurprisingly, therefore, it is packed with gadgets, not least a flying car, and it features evil Baron Bomburst played by Bond baddie, actor Gert Fröbe, Goldfinger himself, and has "Q" taking stage as the village blacksmith.

CCBB has always been a favourite of my family. It certainly was for me as a child – the premiere was in December 1968, just 10 days before my dad died – and I grew up watching it and still love my Corgi toy car with its folding wings (you push the handbrake to make them appear). It's not in perfect nick but neither am I.

Decades later, when Millie and Matt were small, I would sing them the lullaby "Hushabye Mountain", just as Dick Van Dyke, inventor, father and widower Caractacus Potts, does to his kids. Indeed, when asked to come up with alternative names for Millie and Matt for the column, I'd suggested Jeremy and Jemima to Harriet Green at *The Guardian*. She had suggested, rightly, that just maybe these were not entirely contemporary names for 21st-century children…

This love of the film means that it is with a little cry of delight that I push back the desk in my study where a cot once stood and find the lullaby's lyrics, which I'd typed and taped to the wall long ago as a crib sheet to a poor memory. The cot is obviously long gone and I'd thought the hook in the ceiling where a mobile had hung was the last testimony to the sweet, golden days of Matt's babyhood.

There below "Hushabye" are the words for another brilliant *CCBB* tune, "You Too". This one, though, has handwritten corrections to the ending:

> *Could be, we ~~three~~ four get along so famously 'cause you two have ~~me~~ us, and ~~I~~ we have you two, too.*

Finding this would once have reduced me nearly-but-not quite-to-tears and I'd certainly have been cradling a bottle of red wine into bedtime oblivion. Now after the initial shock I break into a broad smile, more grateful for what Helen and I had than sad for what I had lost. Counselling works – thank you again, Heidi. I don't and can't bring myself to change the lyrics back to the original three, though – no one's that strong!

Matt comes up behind me and looks at the sheet:

Matt: *Dad, what's that?*
Me: *Just a song I used to sing to you and Millie.*

He peers more closely at the wall:

Matt: *I remember you singing these. You wouldn't shut up, but it was better than "Me Ol' Bamboo" which was dreadful and you nearly broke the light.*

Matt never forgets anything but he must have been tiny when I, pool cue twirling, did a dad-dance rendition of Van Dyke's finest song. Matt suddenly breaks out in a near shout of enthusiasm:

Matt: *Dad, Dad, you are Caractacus Potts. You so are. You do daft stuff, are always in the garage working on your old car and keep blowing things up. You're him!*

It's true that I spend late evenings, and sometimes the early hours, fixing my old Triumph and my new passion for stained glass has seen some spectacular explosions of glass cooled too quickly from the kiln.

I love the link Matt's making. I've always aspired to Caractacus's optimism and sense of fun – a talented dreamer and in no way a victim of his wife dying and being left an outnumbered grown-up in a chaotic but close threesome.

Nice one, Matt. I can see why the film is even more special to me now Helen has died but why has it always had such enchanted associations for me?

Happy accident or fickle frigging fate, an answer comes only a few days later. It's the sort of coincidence that suggests someone knows Adam has a readership and I've a deadline.

I am in one of my town's brilliant charity shops from which I have furnished my own home, dressed the Yorkshire house into a cosy holiday let and occasionally dressed myself with "dead men's clothes" or DMCs as Helen dubbed them.

Mooching through some of the hardbacks that are always such great value, I spy a white book with an illustrated cover of a racing car and a very enthusiastic driver. I'm unaware of ever having seen it before, but, at the sight of the illustration, I actually squeal with pleasure, much to the surprise of the beige-clad oldie beside me. It is a 1960s edition of *Chitty Chitty Bang Bang*, with beautiful illustrations by John Burningham.

Now I have no memory of my dad, other than of him driving off in his own Chitty, a huge throbbing 1960s Jensen supercar he bought second hand in the year he died. Yet, looking at this unknown but familiar book, I can clearly picture male hands holding it and a male voice reading it aloud. It's my dad reading to me as a child. I know it.

It is such an extraordinarily clear memory. The

emotional rush has me hyperventilating, such that the lady on the till asks:

Lady on till: *Are you all right? You look like you've seen a ghost.*

It's not spectral but special, and happiness overwhelms me as I pay the 99p asking price, plus £20 – it's a fucking Cancer Research shop, hopefully literally.

I love that this has happened. My oldest bereavement is reaching from the past to help me face this terrible new one and build a future for us as I embrace, explosions included, the inner Caractacus in me.

Like him, I am so thankful to have *"someone to care for, to be there for"* in the kids to pull me way from the deep dark hole of grief; we really do get along famously.

38.

NEEDY INDEEDY

Sitting in a café waiting for my date Danielle to arrive is one of the single most stressful things I'd done for years. This may seem madness for a widower to say but online dating in middle age is surprisingly and horribly right up the scale.

I have added reason to be fretting: this is only my third date in more than a quarter of a century and comes after chemistry-free Nicky and Monica and her vicious vulture. It has not been a great start. Online dating really is a stormy sea of hopes and dreams so easily dashed on the craggy rocks of a landscape where certainty and verisimilitude are rarely present or understood. Even if they were they probably wouldn't be spelled correctly. I may be turning into a pedant but it is probably just nerves!

I really need it to be third time lucky as there are more stakeholders this time. Danielle's had been one of the first dating profiles I'd shared with Millie who, with the instinctive forensic ability of a child, had put her finger on an issue that would come to haunt me.

Millie: *Dad, she's lovely. Attractive, must be clever if she's a doctor, possibly too nice for you but I wonder why she's online dating. Something bad must have happened to her in the past, perhaps?*

Me (inattentively as I'm looking at her profile picture thinking how pretty she is): *Yeah, yeah, if you date in your 40s you are going to have lived.*

Danielle and I had been sending one another massive e-mails for weeks, months in fact. Our correspondence had been lengthy, heartfelt, flirty and excitingly scary. Every time we'd asked one another searching questions that required values to be exposed and beliefs shared, the fear was it would be the moment the trapdoor opened. Instead Danielle and I ended up ever more closely connected.

Even then we'd almost run into a low-flying anvil over "The Widower of the Parish" column. When she told me she read *The Guardian*, revealed by her mention of Stella Grey, I realised she'd work out that Adam Golightly was me. This might immediately make her think I'd dated her as a content strategy to report online dating, not as the honest quest for a soul mate that it was.

Danielle and I both suspected that to meet without ever having spoken on the phone was a crazy extra strain on the occasion. So one evening, with the kids in bed, I dialled her number with shaking hands. She sounded lovely and we got on like a house on fire. I ended with:

Me: *I think I should tell you in case you find out later* *that I'm writing a column in the Family section of* The Guardian *about how it is being me aka "The Widower of the Parish".*

Danielle: *Wow. That's unexpected.*

Me: *I wanted to tell you this because if it came out later you'd think I'd hidden it.*

To my emotionally confounded and slightly mad mind I'd found myself worrying that I might lose a woman who would have turned out to be the love of the rest of my life because I was writing cathartically about losing the love of my life (a complex topic as I'll not love Helen any less going forward even if I do meet someone new). Telling Danielle just felt right.

The call had ended well and I went to bed fizzing. This meant I was shocked when I picked up her voicemail message just before leaving for holiday:

Danielle: *I hate to rain on our parade but I'm really uncomfortable that you may be a journalist researching online dating. When you told me about the column, it was like one of those phone messages that cover their backs by telling you that the call is being recorded for training purposes when you know it's much more sinister than that. Sorry but that's it.*

What she was suggesting was so far from the truth. For it to end like this even before anything had really started provoked a greater sense of loss than I could ever have imagined and loss is something I've learned to fear.

Therefore it's not an exaggeration to say that I broke out in a cold sweat.

I called Danielle en route to the airport and simply told the truth – I was no journalist, had no such brief and was dating to start something even if I didn't necessarily know what. She seemed reassured and agreed to meet me on my return. My heart sang, probably too loudly and definitely out of tune with how anyone, never mind a widower, should feel about a woman he has never met.

So it comes that I'm sitting here in Brighton at teatime, having checked into my hotel earlier. I've an overnight pass with in-laws babysitting, only because Danielle and I have talked of dinner if we get on. Navel-gazing nervousness makes me realise that my fears are matched by excitement and overlaid with a touch of guilt. It is a heady brew but a lovely one after so much upset over past months and years.

Danielle walks in. She's beautiful. She also moves with a slender, sensual economy. She's nervous but like me relieved that, for all the good sense that Stella Grey offered, she was talking tosh in our case about the gap between online immersion and physical chemistry. We have buckets of it.

I like Danielle and she likes me. More than that, as I follow her corduroy-clad backside on a wild-goose-chase walk, I really fancy her.

It is one of those sumptuous long afternoons of cherished memories where the sun always shines and for us the conversation and cocktails flowed in equal measure. By six o' clock we are both pleasantly drunk and sharing snacks and stories. Hers is different from mine but no less painful and no less raw given how recently her previous long-term relationship had ended.

Part of me wondered what the hell she was doing dating so soon but the same voice was asking myself the same question, yet here I was. The answer, of course, for me and maybe Danielle, was because part of being a whole human is needing someone to care for, to touch, to adore and be adored by.

I've seen in extreme and dreadful close-up that we come into this world alone and leave it alone, so for me the bit in between craves intimacy in all its guises. OTT, perhaps, but it's how I now feel.

As the light faded we staggered into a fine restaurant and chatted our way through to late evening in what was by then quite a noisy venue. I'd no idea what might happen next and had barely thought about it with my head firmly in the moment. Failing to hear something she'd said with all the surrounding conversation, I leant right in to listen and with no self-consciousness or hesitation we kissed. It felt so natural, maybe because of the booze but more, I think, a celebration and validation of all we had shared over so many weeks. Had we stayed longer, the restaurant would have sold tickets or placed our unseemly middle-aged snogathon on the menu so we grabbed a cab to her cosy village home and fairy-light-lit bedroom.

It was a fabulous end to a first meeting that felt far from a first date because we had shared so much already of our heartache, hopes and dreams.

Over the following weeks we went on to share some more brilliant, gentle, enjoyable times together. There were differences between us that hadn't shown up earlier but I wasn't much bothered by these as our values seemed so aligned. Perhaps I should have been. I think she was still smouldering from the pain of her previous relationship and understandably so. When you've broken up with someone after many years you're looking not to waste so much time again – the burden of proof that you are perfectly matched needs to be desperately high.

We split up some weeks later at Danielle's gentle and honest instigation. I was pretty upset. The truth was I'd become that most undesirable of boyfriends – the needy one. I had a screaming desire to slip back into a cosy loving relationship much like the one I'd lost. The difference, is of course, that that had developed over more than 20 years and could not be dialled back in after a few weeks without me looking desperately and unattractively needy. That I tried to fix her car a couple of times when we should have been dancing the light fantastic says it all.

I had also experienced for the first time the truth of Millie's point about dating in midlife. No one can have sharper pain than a widower or widow but there is something in long-term love lost or unrequited that, incredibly, makes me think that bereavement just may be a more solid foundation on which to build a new life.

Some readers may think I'm wrong to include our story. Danielle was never copy content and when we were together it didn't occur to me that one day I could write about her. That I do so now is because she's a clever, desirable and extraordinary woman. I'll always cherish my relationship with her as my first full and totally immersive one after Helen.

To leave her out of this journey would be to miss a key moment of my grief-resurrection for which I am so grateful to her. There is little defence for my solipsistic mania other than that I really liked her and loved the idea of a fundamental rewrite of the future from sad widower to family man that hooking up with her would mean.

Somewhat guiltily, I put to Heidi this whole business despite it looking more a dating issue than a bereavement one and therefore arguably not within the scope of her remit. She flicked this thought aside while cutting to the chase. I paraphrase a little as it was a long session:

Heidi: *You say how much Helen's death has made you understand how fragile life is so do not want to hang around what could be years.*

Me: *Yes!*

Heidi: *But that is just your model of how life should be and is making you someone who some people will find to their taste but clearly she didn't, which means...*

Me: *... we are not really compatible despite my daring to dream?*

Heidi doesn't answer that question, doesn't need to. I ask an easier one:

Me: *Do you see an idiot before you?*

Heidi: *I see someone whose heart has been broken by his wife dying.*

Another time and with another less raw, less needy and so perhaps more attractive version of myself, I would hope to fall in love with someone like Danielle. I hope she's found happiness, I really do.

39.

PUSSYCAT GALORE

An early column I'd written had been about the joy and furry comfort a cat brought to our family after Helen's death. That joy has not been diminished but augmented by the passing months. Harry, Helen's humungous white Siberian Forest cat, had been her adored pet, and his role as a totem of her life and memory is greater than ever. He is the ersatz fourth family member, a reminder for the kids that their mum was once here too. I am fixated on keeping him alive and ever-present, not just for his sake: I fear terribly telling the children that Harry is lost or worse.

So, while I don't claim a sixth sense, it was with no rational reason that on arriving home one evening I felt an immediate and profound fear for him. I ask Helen's sister Sarah, who brings her sibling's joy and values to the kids by helping me out on Mondays:

Me: *Is Harry in?*
Sarah: *He headed into the garden just before we left for Matt's music lesson.*

I look at the time. It's just over three hours since he has been seen, which is not unusual but the fear is now fully formed and beginning to feel like panic. Once, when Millie was three months old, I left her in her pram at a Post Office. The further I walked, the greater the grip of ill-defined but icy unease. Back at the car, this became a double-handed yank of manic panic as the empty straps of her car seat shouted, "You're a dad now, dickhead." I sprinted back, pursued by hellish visions of loss and calamity that might befall my abandoned baby.

She was fine and I've been lucky not to feel that same cold touch since; until now. I run into the garden, shrilly screaming like a tweeny Potter fan on premiere night:

Me: *Harry, Harry, Harreeeeee!*

Harry should be in the garden. He always is. Not wanting him lost, run over or stolen, when Helen's kitten arrived a few months before she died, I bought a cat fence. There is a radio wire encircling the garden that sends a signal to his collar if he tries to escape. It buzzes ever louder before delivering a small static shock. Like a Pavlov's pussy, he learns to back away at the first buzz, thwarted but unharmed. The scale of shock goes from 1-10 but the salesman had warned us:

Salesman: *Dogs are a five on the shock setting but cats must be 10 – they see a squirrel and go!*

I had visions of a cartoon cat with fur on end but, in practice, it seems less cruel than him being run over or nicked. So Harry is free to roam our roomy garden with its hidey-hole bushes, trees to climb and wildlife to terrorise, gloriously ignoring the breeder's edict when we bought him:

Seller: *Kitten must be a house cat. There's a clause in the contract which requires it.*
Me: *Of course that's fine.*
Me (thinking): *House cat, my arse.*

Once outside, he goes slightly feral in contrast to the furry ball of gentle fun we know indoors. He has been known to wrap his front legs around grey squirrels, dispatching them with raw paw-power, but that aside his time in the garden has been pretty stress-free.

Not today, though. Twenty minutes after my first disquiet we are all out in the rain roaming the area with torches, shining them high into trees like searchlights, hoping for a flash of cat's eyes in return. Nothing.

Ten minutes later I am really panicking and feel sick when suddenly we hear the Tinkerbell toll of a tiny bell. Thankfully it's not a naughty fairy but a very wet, miserably mewing, dishevelled, naughty pussycat.

Harry has become unhappily stranded in a neighbour's garden after making a treetop escape over the radio wire; a newly accessible route probably thanks to his increasing size and strength which allow him to leap greater distances.

The wire's signal had meant he couldn't then return at

ground level but reassuringly he must have stayed close to home, getting ever wetter just outside the signal.

In the neighbour's garden we cuddle and comfort Harry until I take his collar off and he's carried home over the radio wire by an ecstatic Millie and Matt. I follow, almost mute with relief, barely yelping and breaking stride when his special collar, safely tucked in my rain-dampened pocket, picks up the radio signal and zaps my arse hard as I walk too close to the fence. I am also a 10, it seems.

Matt takes stock:

Matt: *Dad, you didn't need to panic. It doesn't help in a crisis.*

I rarely do panic in this way and am a bit shocked myself at how close I was to meltdown. Maybe the intensity of Helen's love for him has made mine that much greater than it should be for a cat, however fabulous. I wonder whether I had somehow picked up and connected with his mewing sadness. Maybe not.

It is certainly ironic, or perhaps fitting, given how supportive Helen had been of my finding a new partner after her death, that Harry's sphere of influence extends outside his wire-fenced prison garden into dating. He is an outstanding online asset, flattering by association the middle-aged schmuck whose profile he sits on.

Almost all my online dating matches "like cats", and Harry inspires easy e-mail banter. Some are chaste, knowledgable observations by enthusiastic women:

Oh, he's blue-eyed with facial marking – a Neva Masquerade then!

Others are baser but fun wordplay of a bawdy sort that Mrs Slocombe from *Are You Being Served?* would approve – she of:

Mrs Slocombe: *Oh, look! It's a diamanté collar for my pussy.*

I discover to my horror that Harry is unafraid to pass judgment on women or rather one woman in particular. Katie was an acquaintance through my old job who lived quite locally and was single and friendly. We had been getting closer but never dated. In town one day she had called and I'd asked her round to the house for the first time for coffee.

As she walked in, instead of Harry's "love me" purring tummy roll, Katie was greeted by an appalling caterwaul he normally reserves for trips in the car to the vet:

Katie: *Oh God. What's up with your cat?*
Me: *I don't know – he's normally so friendly. Harry, stop it!*
Katie (reaching out): *Come on, Harry, what's wrong?*

At this point Harry starts clawing the carpet and swishing his tail menacingly, looking more lynx-like than ever. I flap a little and search for anything to lighten the mood and diffuse the tension:

Me: *Ha! You don't have anything small and furry about your person, do you?*

Katie doesn't answer but throws me a cooler look than I've seen previously. The honeymoon's over even before the wedding.

Later, when Katie has gone and all is calm, I look deep into Harry's brilliant blue eyes asking him:

Me: *Harry – WTF?*

Harry purrs and places a paw on me and I see something mystical. I really do. He's looking out for me, albeit in a rough-and-tumble way. Does even thinking this make me a mad cat man, a weird widower in need of urgent treatment? Harry would say "yes" and in full payback mode probably propose shock therapy.

The legacy of my writing about my screaming fear for Harry's safety is going to be with me for many, many years to come. This is not speculation but fact. Matt, by reading Adam's column about Harry's having gone walk-about, had been fed the insight he needed to start a long-ball game of pet pestering:

Matt: *Dad, can we get another cat?*
Me: *Absolutely not.*
Matt: *Can we say maybe?*

Eventually, of course, I say "yes" to the "maybe" and he ratchets the pressure up with a brilliant sales technique that ropes me in. On a whiteboard one day he sets out his stall – the criteria for selecting the new cat, including:

- Adult
- Female
- At least half Siberian
- Rescue
- Black
- Not too far away

He is an evil genius, as I end up defending my preference for a pedigree Siberian rescue cat and in doing so have somehow accepted the principle of a chum for Harry. I try to beat him at his own game by suggesting that a rescue cat being a pedigree Siberian is about as likely as it also being able to play the piano.

Matt is unrelenting, though, and overcomes a period of inertia on the cat chase by throwing into the mix an argument that I think had been there at the start but he had been reluctant to use:

Matt: *It'll also help you to have another cat.*
Me: *How so? Double the cost to feed, double the vet bills, insurance cost, double the time to look after them when you and Millie leave home.*

Great arguments. None of which touch him:

Matt: *At the moment we are too focused on Harry because he was Mum's cat and you worry so much about anything* *bad happening to him, so having another cat to share our love would dilute that worry for you.*

I'm rendered mute. Millie, who until now has been vociferously against another cat, joins the debate:

Millie: *Dad, he's right.*

As if the fates are listening almost immediately I hear about a six-year-old female pedigree Siberian a breeder is looking to rehouse. I wonder how its paws reach the piano's pedals. There is a catch. She has kittens, one of whom is still with her and available. I agree to let Matt meet them both and he can decide between cat or kitten while I blanch in the corner at the massive cost difference between them. On the day we sit in the breeder's kitchen with a beautiful if run-down silver female and her truly huge ginger kitten. Surprisingly, Matt pays almost no attention to the kitten and sits with the big green-eyed adult cat purring on his lap.

Something isn't quite right so I ask if we can let the breeder know that night. Later I ask Matt:

Me: *You didn't take much notice of the kitten, did you?*
Matt: *No. He was so much more expensive, I don't want it to cost you that much.*
Me: *So do you want us to buy the adult cat?*
Matt: *I did really like her but maybe not this time. Maybe later.*
Me: *Why not? She seemed perfect and it's so unusual to*

find a pedigree Siberian like this. Why not?

Matt: *I don't want to split them up.*

Me: *Oh Matt, it'll happen anyway whether or not we buy her!*

Matt: *It won't be me, though – splitting up the mother from her son.*

I can't quite believe what he is saying and don't have to be Freud to work out what might be going on. Is he manipulating me? I don't think so – his behaviour around the kitten had been real enough. In truth I'm not sure I care if he's putting one over on me or not. Matt has had a tough time and deserves anything I can give him that might bring some more light into his life.

So a few weeks later I'm driving south with two Siberian Forest cats, Luna and Ron, cuddled up asleep in a single basket. At home Millie and Matt await with a very elaborate *Harry Introduction Plan*.

Rather wonderfully, I discover looking at their pedigree forms that Harry and Luna had the same great-grandmother so they are all related, which adds further joy to the familial warmth around their purchase.

Life at home is never going to be the same again but since Helen died it hasn't been the same anyway. Would we ever have had Harry, Luna and Ron if Helen were alive? Probably not, but we would never have needed them if she were here. Now we do, as the kids spotted before and now so do I. Helen, I think, would have done the same and I take Harry's gentle acceptance of his extended furry family as mystic confirmation as he grooms tiny Ron, his second cousin once removed, rather than eating him.

Everyone I tell about having three pets thinks I'm mad. During dads' beer night:

Pete: *Three cats! Are you mad?*

Me: *Meet them. They're lovely.*

Pete: *You joked about this but really now are the mad cat man. You'll be the sort who dies alone eaten by his pets and smelling of wee.*

Me: *People like cats and women in particular seem to love them. You should see how many dating profiles say "Love pets especially cats"!*

Pete: *You're missing the fact that one cat is cute, two is special if you like that sort of thing but three! Three is weird to the point of borderline dysfunctional.*

Chastened, I leave Luna and Ron in the online dating shadows even if one day some as yet unknown candidate for the love of the rest of my life faces a greater challenge than poor Katie. Like a Saturday night talent show contestant, they'll have to try and please not one but three furry-faced judges.

40.

WORLD'S WORST BOYFRIEND

"Do you really think you're ready to be out there dating?"

I have been asked the same question by a number of different friends/relatives/nosey sods in recent months but not as often as I've been asking it of myself, never more so than sitting here alone in the pub.

I hadn't been alone at the start of the evening. With me had been Susan, the fourth woman I'd dated in 26 years, second one I'd actually been out with and my fabulous girlfriend right up to the moment she walked out half an hour ago with the parting shot:

Susan: *You're a fucking animal!*

I sat there shell-shocked, finishing my gin, then drank her untouched one and added a couple more from the bar, trying unsuccessfully to dilute the stream of self-loathing I felt.

Susan and I had been together a few months. After Danielle had brought our relationship to such a swift end, I'd been knocked back for a while; but, as Andy my WAY friend had warned me, the endless possibilities of online dating are like a drug to the lonely soul.

Meeting Susan was once again a case of online attraction converting to brilliant chemistry and some really spectacular dates. Her vivaciousness and dark good looks were matched by a kindness and positivity about her life I found very easy to like. Professionally, she held down a very responsible legal role and seemed to run a large team with ease. She had coped amazingly well with a couple of quite significant setbacks in her life that didn't seem to have made her bitter. This made me feel dreadful for having found a way around her defences and hurt her. Still does.

She'd met the kids, even come to Yorkshire with us, and everyone got on. Susan had become for me kindness, comfort and intimacy in all its guises and as the weeks, then months, passed I felt ever more like a multi-faceted man, not just a widower or dad. To my shame then, I had taken her desire to "talk", which had been the reason to meet that night, as a prompt to seize the nettle of separation rather than advancement.

It was horrible but to have said nothing and played along, giving her false belief in our future together just to avoid conflict would make me a shallow villain of the worst sort. It's not who I am, or at least the man I hope to be.

What I had done, though, clumsy with unhappiness,

nerves and lack of practice in that she was the first woman I'd chosen to split up with since the 1980s, was to allow my focus on saying my piece to make me crassly insensitive to the fact she may have come to the pub with a cherished vision of a future which included a growing love and life with Millie, Matt and me. All of which I had torn up in her face without warning.

Leaving the pub alone, I felt about two inches tall and that night wrote Susan an e-mail to try and better explain what I had been so bad at saying face to face. Then, ignoring the very late hour, I called another WAY friend, Jeannie:

Me: *This hurts more than anything since Helen died. There are even ways in which it is as bad!*

Jeannie: *Are you kidding? How?*

Me: *Helen dying was appalling and the worst thing ever for us all but I was a spectator as fucking cancer controlled events. Here I am the one actively hurting someone I care so much about. It hurts and sucks.*

Jeannie: *So why d'you do it?*

Me: *I was in danger of using her – keeping her as a "girl-friend in a box" to be brought out and played with but in a way that changed nothing else in my life and I'd become pretty sure never would.*

Jeannie: *Is that so bad? You've had a tough ride. It's early days all round. Maybe she was happy to be treated that way – perhaps it suited her in some way that you don't know about.*

I drew a sharp breath. Her implication that it would be in any way OK to string Susan along for my own pleasure because I'd had a hard time was something I hadn't expected her to say and it was shocking. Then again, if your husband had committed suicide your lens on the world would likely be different from pretty much anyone else's. I couldn't let this nonsense go unchallenged.

Me: *Ignoring my certainty I'd hurt her in the future would not just be bad but unkind, which is worse. When Helen died my values didn't go with her, the opposite in fact.*

Jeannie is a bit cool with me after that rather pointed implication that her own values might have shifted south. Either that or I have changed so much myself; to the point of being a sanctimonious prig.

Later that week, I talked through my feelings about Susan with Heidi, unfairly looking for some magical insight and comfort. I asked her what I craved to know – whether it was possible that Susan was the right person at the wrong time.

Me: *Does bereavement, grief, guilt or whatever mean I'm incapable of falling in love with anyone this month, year, ever?*

Heidi's response as ever underlines that she is a counsellor and will not be pushed into acting as a clairvoyant.

Heidi: *You have talked about Susan a lot and aired your fears about keeping her in a box. That itself tells you something, maybe everything, about the relationship.*

Me: *Like what?*

Heidi: *You already know.*

Of course I do and in truth I suspect, smart as she is, Susan will have worked it out too, that somehow my subconscious links love to the screaming pain of Helen's death and any steps I take towards it, however small, hurt too much and maybe always will.

The positivity and fairness of Susan's subsequent reply to my e-mail was by some distance kinder than I deserved. I can only hope I have not turned to vinegar her memories of the special times we enjoyed together.

Since Helen died I have dated and had immersive relationships – any of which in different circumstances, with a different version of me, might have lasted. Too many? Not enough?

I feel ever more like a child running wildly around the park with arms flung wide open, looking to hug and be held. In my case it's a simple craving to find new happiness in terms of love in all its beautiful forms. Am I likely to keep on hurting others when I already know that I'm like a car that cannot get into top gear emotionally because when last it happened there was a massive, terrible crash in which a limb was lost? Susan hadn't even asked where we were going or demanded anything but I'd anticipated the change and braked hard on our relationship. What a twat.

My worry is that I may never be able to go there again and worse still will hurt others finding this out. At least the "others" do not include Millie and Matt. I protect them as much as I can – no women has or any time soon will share my bed at home because it would literally be Helen's space. I also try to avoid making up the magic number four round the table at mealtimes.

Even so I know that things are a bit surreal because when sounding out the kids about my dating, they don't hold back:

Me: *How do you feel if I start online dating again?*

Matt (smiling): *We'd not worry about it. It would only matter if you were going to marry someone, and anyway…*

Me: *Anyway, what?*

Matt (now laughing): *They wouldn't be around in a few months anyway, Dad.*

Oh God. He's joking but it's humour plastered over truth. It's some appalling role reversal. Millie has only ever had one boyfriend and they have celebrated their first-year anniversary; Matt's at a very casual six-month anniversary with his girlfriend. And their dad?

I'm not one of those apocryphal "recent" widowers who fast-track through dating into rapid remarrying – in stark contrast to the many years widows seem to remain alone. Maybe the facets of my persona which help me nurture the kids also act as a break on my ability to commit, despite my being out there dating with the stereotypical urgency of recently bereaved blokiness. Surely this makes me a horrible hybrid, dating but destined to be a serial bearer of angst and upset? Thinking of Susan's expression as she left, I ask myself unhappily out loud whether she was right:

Me: *Am I indeed a fucking animal after all?*

I don't like the sound of this at all and look for help. With no Heidi in the frame, it's a shame Pete is away on the sort of business trip with clients that will have him back with a tan, carrying a little more weight and a set of golf clubs. This doesn't matter, though, because I think it would do no harm to get a woman's eye view on this, the last dating debate I want to have for a while.

So it's with my local sensible and definitely female people watcher Laura that I sit in a local tapas bar and share several small plates and one big question:

Me: *Am I out of control?*

She has just listened to me giving her 20 minutes of context and, with a look that is quizzical, asks something which would make Pete proud:

Laura: *Would you mind lifting your shirt up at the front a little?*
Me: *What?*
Laura: *Do it, please.*

Me: *Why?*

She doesn't answer and I think what the hell and lift it.

Laura: *A little higher.*

I obey until there are a few inches of hairy stomach that may or may not be putting people off their own small plates on surrounding tables.

Laura: *OK, that's fine.*

I lower my shirt.

Me: *What was that all about?*
Laura: *I just wanted to give someone else a chance to gaze at your navel since you've clearly been doing so much of it yourself.*
Me: *Euugh, that's cheesy.*

We look at one another in silence until one of us breaks and we both laugh out loud causing the table to rock.

Laura: *You need to laugh about this as you are beating yourself up so much and you shouldn't be. Seriously, you're in danger of driving yourself mad.*
Me: *But I've screwed up – any one of the women I've met could have been "the one".*
Laura: *Or none of them. Or more interestingly, all of them.*

Me: *All of them!!!*

Laura: *Yes. It's possible but the fact that you are not with them means you simply weren't ready for it to happen – too busy, too choosy, too needy, too pushy, too scarred, too... broken-hearted.*

Unsurprisingly, her echoing of Heidi's turn of phrase adds weight to my attention to and consideration of what she's saying.

Me: *But it has caused so much pain for everyone. Should I just become a monk?*

Laura: *Think about it this way – maybe you needed to have been through all this just to come out the other side in a better place. You were with Helen for so so long and suddenly find yourself out there, unaccountably attractive to women looking for a serious hook-up without a bloody clue what you are doing or are ready for. All of this dating pain may have needed to happen before you come safely in to harbour on the other side of your grief.*

I let a few moments pass and exhale loudly:

Me: *But what about the women I've been out with and those I may date in future while in this state; do I have to put them through this too?*

Laura: *Ask yourself how you'll ever find the "other side" of grief. It's not by sitting at home grooming cats. It seems you are doing your best to avoid or at least minimise the* *pain for anyone daft enough to be your girlfriend, and if the kids are fine with it then count your blessings and stop overthinking things. Stay healthy, and embrace the fact that another life partner is not an easy quest and certainly not won just by refreshing a bleeding dating page. And of course there's the elephant in the room...*

I cannot help raising the one eyebrow I can raise, Roger Moore style.

Laura: *Of all the pain you are fretting about none of it gets even in the same book, never mind the same page as yours in losing Helen. You are rebuilding a totally flattened normality after 26 years. Causing someone some upset after a few months because you don't want to hurt them more isn't the same pain, it's more a harsh inconvenience for them.*

Thus Laura offers me absolution and makes fair points. I won't let myself too far off the hook when it comes to causing pain to others – tempting though it is. But I can live with myself, I think, and hopefully am emerging through this stage of my journey.

I've always known that I have a huge capacity for love but have discovered I've an even greater need for it. I've indulged it and don't feel great about that. I'm no masochist but remind myself that love and hate often travel on the same train.

41.

COFFEE CONFIDENTIAL

I'm drinking coffee alone in *Costbucks* no more than a couple of feet away from three sporty-looking Lycra-clad women chatting at the next table. They're talking unselfconsciously and fairly loudly as they chew the fat in lieu of burning it off. But then who am I to throw stones as I tuck into my Victoria Sponge and Latte combo.

Their volume is such that I can track the topics of conversation – house prices, schools, spouse's job and children's achievements with the occasional hushed report of someone else's epic lifestyle fail. All of this comes my way through incomplete sentences as their voice levels eddy depending on the juiciness of topic. Even as an unwilling listener it can be frustrating not to hear clearly some of the more edgy-sounding story arcs:

> *A term behind on school fees…been seeing someone behind her back…in a nightdress. …head to toe in jelly…*

I wasn't listening intentionally or being particularly

judgemental about their gossiping. Not, that is, until my own surname (subbed by Golightly here) pricked up and then syringed my ears into suddenly hearing almost every word:

Lycra 1: *Adam Golightly seems to be coping pretty well after Helen.*
Lycra 2: *Yes, he's done brilliantly and Millie and Matt seem so well but...*

About now I should have identified myself or left, having heard enough to feel momentarily good but also knowing from experience what would follow, given the *flatter before flattening* nature of small-town gossip. I hesitated, and then sat still, far too nosey for my own good.

Lycra 2: *...he may well be getting over it but does he really need to live out his second childhood in front of them?*

How did they not see me sitting so close? Perhaps because of the invisibility suit I was wearing. It was not some fabulous magical material lined with stars and fairy dust nor a technological marvel of micro cameras and perspective management. It was a simple pair of blue workman's overalls, slightly grubby from a morning in the glass studio rebuilding and cementing a large panel. Wearing these should see me stand out a mile in this town's coffee shops, populated as they are generally by MacBook jockeys typing and yummy mummies mingling. Yet my workwear is a brilliant disguise, making me a tradesman so perceived as occupying a different social stratum and therefore totally invisible to the usual coffee-house coterie.

They don't see me but I do recognise one of the three, gathered as they are around the bubbling cauldron of my reputation. I neither know her name nor have we ever spoken but I have seen her face around for years. She must have had a child in Millie's year at primary school. The second woman's more damning voice is unknown to me, which is troubling given she is so scathingly opinionated. The third member of the tittle-tattle triumvirate guzzles coffee silently, no doubt enjoying the briefing, probably taking notes.

I try to rise above it and sip my coffee, turn my head away and tune out. Despite this, a few keywords slip through: "no job", "new house", "girlfriends", "stained glass", "new car" "seeing Jo".

Hearing my self-declared sister-in-loss Jo's name is too much. I had wondered at the time, whether our very platonic friendship so soon after Helen's death might cause rumours but am stunned that it's still a conversational currency. How the buggery do they know these things? Is there a newsletter? Does being a small-town widower bring macabre celebrity? I cock an ear this time, on tenterhooks for where it might go next:

Lycra 1: *It's classic midlife crisis stuff.*
Lycra 2: *Yeah. Bit old for it, though, isn't he?*

They laugh.

Midlife crisis? No shit, Sherlock! How much more of a midlife crisis can you have than your beautiful wife/kids' mother dying before your eyes of a rare fucking cancer? As for "over it" – deep breaths and full glasses of Bordeaux were required when I wrote this up for Adam's column on what would have been Helen's birthday.

Even sitting there I realised my rage was out of all proportion with what these women were saying. A few months previously the raging anger I'd felt after I'd knocked car park wanker Warren to the ground had led to the calm counselling of Heidi, who made me understand that the problem was more mine than his. Likewise these lycra-clad women are largely innocent as they fill their tanks with inflammatory gossip, not realising the car is already ablaze.

I move tables to get thankfully out of earshot, and there distract myself with the thought of "second child-hood" which resonates with something I had just read and taken comfort from. Until recently, it was believed that adults, unlike children, could not develop new brain cells. Now it's thought that in certain circumstances new neurons can grow at any age (neurogenesis).

The neuroscientist Dr Sandrine Thuret identifies neurogenesis as a natural state but one undermined by stress, lack of sleep, alcohol, diet and, of course, ageing. This lack of new cells can anchor people in depression – cancer patients, for example, whose medication prevents neuron growth remain depressed even after the "all clear".

Stress, related to bereavement, can undermine

neurogenesis and, while grieving is important as you don't need a psychologist to tell you, it should probably not be too deep or too long lest it becomes normalised and hard-wired into your lifestyle. The battleground for all this is the brain's hippocampus, linked to moods and emotions.

The upside of the new knowledge, according to Thuret, is that anyone can provoke neuron growth through three key drivers – body, mind and heart. The road back from grief, then, might include exercise, learning new things and close physical and emotional contact – love being the gold standard.

It's probably why most kids cope relatively well with bereavement. Millie's and Matt's fast-growing lives mean they are maxing out on all three dimensions, with the importance of love vindicating my continual presence by packing up my job. They are also, of course, producing neurons effortlessly due to their youth. For someone like me who is bereaved and a "bit old" (thank you lycra lady 2), neurogenesis can be a "target of choice", says Thuret, if we want to "improve decline associated with ageing and stress". To increase the production of neurons, we need to access positive growth factors such as running, a healthy diet, red wine, chocolate and sex.

I've been out running lots, drinking gallons of red wine, guzzling giant chocolate buttons, much to the kids' dismay, and indulged my riotous libido a bit. Is it possible that my relative positivity in coping with the dreadful world which no longer has Helen in it, is because inadvertently I've been pursuing a path littered with prime neuron growth factors? Perhaps my bereaved brain had just been lucky in pursuing the very factors that might help alleviate my grief or perhaps my mind is using some underutilised capacity to subconsciously pursue them.

Either way in this scenario grief has been the architect of my behaviour, driving me to gratify body, mind and heart and, as it turns out, brain 'n' all. I like to think so, telling it to no one in general but myself in particular to help quell any doubts that I'm getting this bereavement stuff right.

If this is the case why doesn't every bereaved person behave like me? Possibly because writing Adam's column has forced me to navel-gaze my motivations in a way that never usually happens so soon to those who have loved and lost. Being paid weekly to eviscerate one's emotions doesn't half force you to work through survivor's guilt and section grief into bite-sized, just-about-digestible chunks. I believe that with Adam I have possibly fast-tracked the grieving process. I have experienced it no less deeply or darkly than others on this journey but perhaps more broadly – death, life, sex, anger, joy and excess have characterised the past few months and somehow made me more alive and positive than others in the same timeline.

I'm not exhorting other bereaved people to necessarily have a midlife crisis but I am saying don't be upset or guilty if you desire your own grief resurrection – your subconscious brain may be calling the shots, hungry for neurons. Why not let it loose? Just make sure you put any kids first, don't do drugs and try better than I have not to hurt anyone – nothing else really matters.

42.

CRYING DOWN TO RIO

O ne of the more surprising questions to come my way was from an absolute stranger whose right to have asked it in the first place was questionable but I am glad he did.

Stranger: *Do you miss your wife?*

It's such a simple thought, so personal and the answer so bleeding obvious that no one has asked it since the day Helen died. Not having been asked doesn't mean not having thought about it and I had done so a lot since first reading CS Lewis on the subject. The answer therefore flowed from me easily and without drama, my voice low but as insistent as the rain-spangled breeze which rustled the trees above the two of us, sharing as we were a simple wooden park bench.

Me: *It was an amputation. Helen was here and now she isn't but is ever present in her absence. Amputees sometimes get*

pain in the missing limb as do I in moments of inactivity,
when her presence seems almost within touching distance,
which makes it all the worse that she isn't.

Stranger: *And that's why you are always running around*
doing stuff and creating the need to do even more stuff?

Me: *You know that one? May I ask how?*

Stranger: *My wife. Cancer, Twenty years ago.*

Me: *It gets better?*

Stranger: *Different. Bearable and always there despite so*
much well-intentioned advice to the contrary.

He smiled. I smiled in return. Somewhat surreally, we
were sitting in what I assumed was some sort of garden of
remembrance outside the county crematorium. I had just
attended a service for the father of a close friend, Charlotte.
He had died unexpectedly and although I had only met
him a few times, I felt I needed to be there to support
her and her family. I had faced the idea of attending
with a growing dread, which until now I had kept to
myself. It was the same crematorium where 10 of us had
said goodbye to Helen's mortal self before her large-scale
remembrance service back at the local church. Today I'd
arrived and parked up around the corner, hanging back,
and had just made it in before the start but after the coffin
had entered, which is bad form. Fortunately her father's
achievements were such, as I was soon to discover in a very
moving and probably the most celebratory crem service I
have ever attended, that the place was packed and I was
able to join surreptitiously the overflow on the large upper
balcony. Thankfully it was a different chapel from the one

in which we had placed our individual flowers on Helen's wicker coffin, and this had helped me calm down. By focusing on the sincerity of the beautiful service, I got through it and felt I'd faced my fears well.

Afterwards we all first assembled outside for hellos and hugs prior to heading off to a local golf club for refreshments. The grief ambush came as I realised we were in the same garden as we had been for Helen – an appalling wave of sadness washed over me. I fought back, hugging friends and dragging up humour about the chaos that is my private life but it was no good, I had to leave before becoming a distraction to someone else's deep grief.

First to leave, I walked off quickly, only to see the assembled funeral director's cars waiting outside. I saw immediately that it was the same firm we had chosen for Helen; even the hearse had the same personalised registration as the decrepit Rolls Royce that had gassed Millie, Matt and me as we walked behind it, but it was now on a much newer vehicle. It was a stupid thing to notice but it was the final straw.

I literally ran into the grounds and sat on a bench to gather myself. That was where, after a few minutes, I'd been joined by this calming, kind stranger sharing his experiences as a fellow, more experienced traveller – not least how to deal with the unsolicited well-meant advice that the bereaved get in abundance. So of course I asked him:

Me: *And your advice to me?*

He answered in his slow, well-spoken voice with just the faintest trace, I think, of an American accent, one that suggested he had been outside the US for a long time:

Stranger: *Those frustrating moments when you stop charging around and it's as if she's almost back with you, they don't have to be bad. They can, if you slow down enough to properly embrace them, be moments of connection that you'll cherish, not fear.*

I look into his eyes and see nothing but certainty and serenity and feel wash over me a teary calmness which I last felt watching Rio Ferdinand's *Being Mum and Dad* documentary, something that had transformed from an obstacle to avoid to a memory to treasure.

The film is a fly-on-the-wall view of Rio Ferdinand's quest to understand the grief process following his wife Rebecca's early death in 2015, also from fucking cancer – more specifically, how he could guide his three children to find a means to "...talk happily and be joyful about their mum rather than it being sad and negative..."

The parallels in our stories, I suppose, had prompted a few radio stations to get in touch with Adam when the film was due to be aired, asking him/me to join panel discussion programmes. I had previously chosen to accept these invitations, glad to add to a wider audience's understanding of the journeys of the invisible bereaved who live among them, silently and often alone in coping with their grief.

Despite this desire to contribute and the added fact of

it being an even newer discussion of the hitherto hidden truths of being a widower dad, somehow I found myself wanting to duck it. I didn't but it had been a good instinct as immediately after taking part it all returned – the profound unfairness of Helen's death, her missing Millie and Matt's growing up and countless barbs of misery and fear tearing at the newly formed skin covering the wound of Helen's amputation from our lives. I'd had my fill of misery.

So come the broadcast, I didn't watch and in reply to the question "did you see Rio Ferdinand?", I simply shook my head, provoking versions of:

> *"Don't watch it, mate! It'll be too much."*
> *"Too painful."*
> *"You're just forward and it'll send you backwards!"*

More rationally, I also wondered whether a story of a wealthy celebrity's grief could have any relevance to mine. Would it simply be a grand demonstration that money can massage misery and privilege prevent pain?

Then, by chance, I saw Rio quoted in connection with the Government's proposal to limit bereavement benefit to only two years for new widows or widowers. I was outraged by its moral bankruptcy, and driven by my newly found, grief-formed compassion, wrote a column encouraging readers to complain to their MP.

The link to the pro-forma letter of objection received a big upsurge and I supported the cause in social media as well. It was a very bitter taste when the bill was passed by MPs with their golden-parachuted, expense-accounted and index-linked pensions. It was a cause that mattered to me and so it really hit home to see Rio reported as saying:

Rio Ferdinand: *If I'm honest, I don't understand how the Government can actually say there's a timescale on it because there is no timescale on anything to do with bereavement. There isn't a time when you can say, "Yeah, I'm over it." Putting a number on it is the wrong thing to do.*

With these words, which so mirror my own, Ferdinand the man, not the personality, came alive to me. And, with a clear space in the diary and a beer to hand, I watched the documentary about his experience, and found it totally and tragically compelling. So many touch-points beyond the obvious ones of disease, logistics and love.

His shock at Rebecca's diagnosis and sense of betrayal at the speed of her death; his recognition of thoughts of suicide without ever going close to it because of the impact on the kids; his difficulty in watching videos of Rebecca even for the kids' sake all connected with me through the screen and bridged differences of background, profile and age. He shares my journey because I know his.

I found myself recognising all too closely his sense of a "fully loaded diary" as a means of grief avoidance and, not least, the sense that "filming has been therapy for me". Substitute "writing" for "filming" and I'm in there.

The only jealousy that the film provoked was not of fabric but of feelings – Ferdinand cried tears of memory and in doing so was clearly far further into the grieving process than I was. I have longed to cry yet hadn't in any meaningful way... until then. Fuelled perhaps by the build-up, I cried tears of grief and loss for the first time since Helen's diagnosis. I did so at his story in a way that I could never do for my own lest I lost the control and strength that Millie and Matt and others needed from me. Yet the touch-points meant my tears for him were also, and at last, for Helen too.

I meant it when I ended the column with the thought that every bereaved father should watch this documentary, perhaps retitling it *"Rio Ferdinand: Mum, Dad and Widower of the Nation".*

It was with no small pleasure, therefore, that I heard from his agent's office some weeks later – Rio, they told me, had read the column and seen it as one of the best he'd seen on the subject, and asked for a hard copy for his children's memory book. Of course I'm gratified that someone so well known should have read my piece but more than that it made me understand just how much I'd begun to hope that my widower writing genuinely helped people who have experienced love and loss and that it did not just entertain, amuse or annoy them.

Back at the crematorium I wanted to leave before the rest of the mourners might pass us, so I said goodbye:

Me: *I just want to thank you for... for everything.*
Stranger: *It was a pleasure to talk to you. My wife is here and I come often but rarely get to chat. Thank you.*

Walking off in the rain towards the car, I got about 100 yards before I realised that I'd left the small umbrella I'd borrowed from Millie's school bag in the chapel. Turning around, I was more than a little surprised to see that the bench was now empty. I froze, rooted to the spot, scanning with my eyes in all directions but I couldn't see him anywhere.

It played out like a film as I arrived at a goose-bumped conclusion that my calming, caring friend, who'd sat with me surrounded by the remains of those who once lived, may no longer himself have been of this world. This made it frankly something of a relief when a few minutes later, having abandoned any idea of retrieving my brolly as another service had started, I saw his very mortal, extraordinarily sprightly figure exiting the gents by the garden. I thank the stars for that – good though his advice was and glad as I am to have received it, there are enough observers on my journey dispensing guidance without adding a supernatural stakeholder to their count.

43.

SURVIVE AND THRIVE

"I open at the close," says the message hidden in the Golden Snitch, revealed only as the threads of Harry's story are woven together in the final Potter book. Helen's great love of these stories made it an inspiring maxim for my final "Widower of the Parish" column.

While my writing was never intended as a guidebook, the very last "Widower of the Parish" column was called "How to Survive the Death of a Loved one" and shared some gentle suggestions to help others. I saw them as key topics and top tips that books on grief and bereavement tend not to mention, friends dare not suggest and the bereaved don't have the time or inclination to stare into space and think about.

Looking at each one afresh now, I realise that some of them were very specific tips, only relevant to those who are grieving. I have no hesitation in repeating versions of these as good advice now, not least because the response to that last column was so overwhelmingly positive.

If you are a fellow bereaved traveller you could do worse than look at:

Appendix A: 10 Step Guide to Surviving Bereavement

I am far from an expert and no grief counsellor. All I can say is these worked for me and still largely do.

Someone smarter than I might determine how they work in theory and apologies in advance to anyone who may think them statements of the bleeding obvious or somehow heretical to "normal" grieving patterns.

However, if you've come this far you'll understand that I have sought for my own sake and that of Millie and Matt not just to survive but even to find a new happiness that accepts grief and builds on it.

I realise that over the months my embracing of the massive change of Helen's death has opened my eyes to much that was unknown or hidden in full view. As never before I understand playwright Dennis Potter's ability to see the "nowness" of everything that I wrote about early in the book (see "Mindfulness Shmindfulness"). Through the lens of his own fucking cancer and only a few months from death, he could see the beauty in the world around as never before within the narrowing boundaries of the life he had left.

I don't for a minute claim parity at any level with Dennis Potter and hopefully have more than a few weeks of life left to me but unexpectedly and amid all its darkness and grief, Helen's death has given me one last great gift. This final one was brought about by my close proximity to her endless courage, humour and zest for life from diagnosis to death and is her greatest legacy to me (other than the kids!) – a lens through which to look at the world as Dennis Potter did, as if it were my last few weeks upon it:

Dennis Potter: *It's a plum tree, it looks like apple blossom but it's white, and looking at it, instead of saying "Oh that's nice blossom"... last week looking at it through the window when I'm writing, I see it is the whitest, frothiest, blossomest blossom that there ever could be, and I can see it.*

It took months, following Helen's diagnosis, for me to truly see the glory of what Potter calls "nowness" – its lens being honed initially by our taking pleasures where we could as we held tight to normality and fought the closing boundaries of what we could do as a family. After she died this new view became clouded by grief, shock, logistics and emotional mayhem but all of these have been normalised enough now to allow me a clear line of sight again on this beautiful world as I never could see it before – and with it the chance to live in a way that has more meaning, more direction and greater happiness.

It is a gift that I wish I had been given years ago, but one that came at too high a price of course... and therein lies a Catch 22 which really troubles me.

This is in Sherlock Holmes parlance a "two-pipe problem" but in Pete's probably a four-pint one and it is to him I go, having spent a bit of time working out how best to articulate my disquiet – over a dinner à deux in a relatively upmarket restaurant:

Pete: *Does this mean we're dating? Such a surprise!*

Me: *Ha bloody ha! I need your advice on something that's troubling me. There are avenues I want to travel in the book which feel maybe wrong or even dangerous to explore but are still part of my journey.*

Pete (gazing at the menu): *Dangerous like a fat bloke on a doctor's warning in a pie shop?*

I ignore Pete's banter, wanting to offload my thoughts on him asap. I am really tortured that it is only because Helen died that I have experienced and learned so much that I would never otherwise have done; stuff which may make me a better father, friend and man. How should that make me feel? I pitch straight in:

Me: *Bereavement has given me great insight into myself and life in general, stuff that I now realise I wish I'd known years ago. Stuff that would have shaped for the better how Helen and I had lived before she fell ill. Would living it, sharing it, be disloyal to the memory of the life Helen and I lived and loved together?*

A tough brief for Pete, but one it turned out did not require a swanky dining room, fine wines and the three hours I'd allowed for this consultation. He nailed the issue and presented a solution in about two minutes. To add insult to the heavy hit on my wallet, he did so by lecturing me using my own writing as a prop:

Pete: *You made the point yourself in one of Adam's*

columns, which gave us a slightly contrived allusion to a Shakespearian "sea change"- The Tempest? Ariel?

Me (hesitatingly, not rising to bait): *Yeeees?*

Pete: *You then talked about yours being a C change in which the C was, as I think you are accustomed to say, "fucking cancer". Your journey is actually about very little else but* change *so why wouldn't you talk now about the change you aspire to* for yourself and others.

Me: *Because it would be strange claiming Helen's death has empowered me like this – like insight being presented by a man in a black frock coat, top hat and carriage with black-plumed horses.*

Pete gives me a look suggesting the head waiter would have understood better what he had said (certainly he was now speaking loudly enough):

Pete: *People avoid change, as did you until you had no choice and Helen died. You've learned a lot because of it and can write it down because Adam needed you to. If any person who might read your words, bereaved or not, could end up in a better place, you should share your experience – separate the fact that* change *can result in good things from the reason in your case for change being a dreadful one – ie fucking cancer.*

Me (strident, almost angry): *What! You mean present Helen's death just as… as… as an agent of change? I'm not that strong and how would it sound for…*

Pete: *…Pete's sake!*

Me: *…fuck's sake!*

We look at one another and laugh. He's magically lightened the mood of a sticky moment: have he and Laura been comparing notes?

Pete: *Look, you're writing a book that's about your new life but it's hardly light on reporting your love of Helen. A love that is as obvious today as it was singing "Mr Blue Sky" at her funeral, mainly because far from wearing a frock coat, you're looking more like a tramp every day.*

Me: *What?*

Pete: *That shirt is one Helen bought you, isn't it? You've a few of them, all frayed and with trousers the arse is hanging out of, a jumper that's so worn it looks like it's flown through a plague of moths. Helen bought them all?*

I hadn't realised this but he's right. I'm wearing and not replacing the last clothes Helen bought me, not wanting to literally cut the thread on that connection. Pete's a smart man in a posh restaurant with a friend who looks like a tramp, but at least one whose eyes have been opened by this conversation.

It is why now I can look beyond life-enhancing tips that are grief-specific towards those that have a wider audience of anyone looking to improve their lot in life. These are the sorts of thing I have heard over the years from self-help books and life coaches which sounded fine in theory but I never applied well enough because they required too much change, and change is pretty scary. Well, now the massive forced change of loss and my journey to rebuild around it have given me a much better understanding of the application and prioritisation of these behaviours.

At the end of the book are quite simply my thoughts on living a happier life. I wish I'd had this insight and the courage to apply it years ago, when Helen was alive and would have benefited from a better version of me. This is your chance, no strings attached; no one else had to die to get them:

Appendix B: 10 Ways Anyone Can Be Happier

That's it. Just 10 exercises. These will get you en route to being happier with the time you have left on earth. Surely anyone can have a crack at 10?

I'm not, nor do I wish to be, a life coach, but who knows, maybe a few steps well taken are worth more than a bucket of books or a cascade of courses. Be warned and be better than I am – I would certainly never have had this insight or courage enough to embrace change if the decision hadn't been taken for me by fucking cancer killing my wife and forcing my hand. As I said so long ago at the start, if not a life coach then maybe I'm a death coach, qualified only to help people live the life they'd love, which may not be the one they have.

44.

MOVING ON WITHOUT LEAVING BEHIND

With the end of the column in sight, I had mixed feelings. The insistent weekly requirement to deliver a taut 700 words was quite onerous, given my sole adult-in-charge domestic chaos, much as I really enjoyed writing it – a new thing! There was also a voice in my head wondering whether "The Widower" was somehow anchoring me in grief.

Thankfully, as so often since Helen died, my still small inner voice was again talking balls.

Being Adam Golightly has been truly cathartic for me in opening the door on my sadness and forcing me to confront demons even before they became destructive. I've been able to share with family and friends events around Helen's death that would never otherwise have been spoken of, not because I wouldn't have wanted them to be heard but because the pace of coping and working on the reconstruction of our lives left no natural space for introspection and analysis.

Also towards the end, the status of being a "*Guardian*

columnist" was a real confidence boost, beating hands down "unemployed, possibly unemployable, bereaved, middle-aged, once upon a time media man" – it offered a stable platform for a rebuild.

A further thumbs-up came from Helen's ever-supportive sister Sarah who told me something totally unexpected and fantastically lovely:

Sarah: *Don't you realise, with all you've said and done, you've pulling the rest of the family through?*

I hadn't even vaguely seen this, thinking instead I was running the risk of inadvertently sharing too much too soon and alienating everyone. My being wrong about all these things has been an almost laughably consistent feature of my grief journey.

Thanks to social media I have had some sense that others were taking comfort from the column. I'd decided to include a Twitter address, @MrAdamGolightly, once the column was up and running, despite some concerns by Harriet's team that I might get abuse. In fact, I feel blessed, as there was immediately an amazingly positive response and only a couple of negatives from women who were bereaved themselves and therefore perfectly entitled to their opinion. Their beef was largely, I think, that my journey was not the same shape as theirs – drunker, ruder, quicker. Finding one another, they threw a few 140-character bricks Adam's way. When these comments had escalated to become especially hurtful, another member of the community, Jen from Cork, waded in to my defence, which was very kind and led to a friendship, which still endures.

Funnier were some early refusals to believe that I exist:

I suspect you are a Guardian *journalist or a group of them. These things simply don't happen in real life!*

Curiously, I found this really pleasing – not just that I would be mistaken for a professional writer but as a validation of why I started writing in the first place. So many of my experiences seemed genuinely richer, more bizarre, more coincidental than any fiction.

Even more pleasing was that a number of accomplished, published writers have chosen to follow Adam, including those who actually teach creative writing. Perhaps they know I need help!

It was lovely and occasionally scary to have such informed scrutiny. From my early days of always having a buffer of four columns ready to go, it dwindled to just three, then two, then one until I was writing literally only a week ahead. With a greater sense of scrutiny, I had put more pressure on myself for it to be a rewarding read and they were taking longer to craft (vs. bang 'em out at the outset). Often it was taking longer to write a column than to live the events they were reporting.

Over the weeks I'd developed a new Saturday morning routine. I'd tweet the column first thing in the morning when it came out, then would sit reading the paper in "Costbucks" while waiting for the kids to finish their swimming and karate. I enjoyed watching positive replies and "likes" pop up over the hour or so as I was sitting there. It was a gentle, relaxing ritual in a busy week made occasionally pleasantly surreal when I would see someone else reading it around me.

I mentioned this to my friend "red" Robin over a cheeky beer; a psychologist whom I purposely avoided speaking to about my problems exactly because he is a friend, and anyway I have Pete – less qualified but more approachable because of it. Robin sat back in his chair, took off his glasses and rubbed his distinctly gingery beard before giving me a very sharp look and asking with a clinical cadence:

Robin: *How do you feel after reading the social media stuff?*

I looked at him, surprised at my mate's transformation into his professional persona:

Me: *Great. Really great. It's lovely!*
Robin: *How long does this last for?*
Me: *For days or at least until something goes pear-shaped. I sort of bounce my way into writing the next column because of it.*
Robin: *You keep saying how the pace of your coping seems almost indecently, disloyally quick; well, my friend, you may just have found out why.*

Robin had seen that not only was writing the columns therapy in itself but also how much this weekly glad-handing in social media was accelerating the rate at which I was dealing with grief.

He's indeed a clever gingery bloke and he asked whether he could write something up in a professional journal about me, to which I agreed, as long as it's after the book comes out and he doesn't name the man.

Thinking back, when the Twitter feed went live, my sense of purpose and validation of my journey did seem to gain pace – not just because of the obvious support for the controversial stuff, like Lucy between the sheets, but far more importantly because of the positivity with which people saw my nurturing of Millie and Matt. Unexpected and fantastic – thank you.

Personal messages on Twitter further suggested Adam's words were doing some good as people shared their own challenges. I found it impossible to ignore them and wanted to help, writing back and even meeting a couple of followers. Among the several I would count as friends today, there's Heather in her late 30s, with tiny children whose husband also died of fucking cancer. She's slowly rebuilding a day at a time but is remarkably positive and upbeat in the blog she writes and the life she lives. She opens up to me one to one finding it easier to talk to a fellow traveller because:

Heather: *...don't you find it gets to the point where you think people don't always want to hear about the down days?*

So it is for me too and I have some really positive, engaging online dialogue with her as a result.

And then Penny, whose husband is very much alive but has his own form of probably incurable fucking cancer. Penny has been so supportive of my journey while sharing her own 'black hole" moments about her fear of a future alone bringing up her kids once the worst happens:

Penny: *And there really aren't that many people I can say that to explicitly. I think you may well be the first!*

I feel both privileged and occasionally fearful that I tread too heavily or come across in the column's edited highlights of my real rounder, duller life as a bit of a tosser. So far either they are being kind or there is indeed a hard-wired bond between those who are bereaved, and the bereaved-in-waiting. This bond allows us to be pretty robust and down to earth with one another about love, death, sex, grief and pain, all expressed in a way that rarely sees light of day in the mainstream media. This is possibly the very reason another Twitter mate, Carol, messaged me:

Carol: *My husband's dying of fucking cancer. I can't tell anyone about mourning the loss of my love life amongst the thousand other heartaches, no matter how true or symbolic it is of everything being taken away from us. Wrong. People would say nothing but think "selfish bitch".*

It's interesting also that while I have always called fucking cancer "fucking cancer"; no one has ever suggested it's wrong to swear about it. Penny, like most of my Twitter folk, played it back to me unselfconsciously:

Penny: *It's a tough gig for the realistic optimist, this bastard fucking cancer.*

Actually, if anyone reads this who works for one of the big cancer research players and wants some help fundraising, there's tons of scope for a swear-box-based campaign wherein people pay for the privilege of calling fucking cancer by its true sweary name. I've mentioned this before but am more certain than ever that swearing about cancer gives people a release they would pay for and I'd happily work with any charity whose balls are big enough to embrace the idea. Together we need to beat the fucker and desperately need that money.

Twitter also made me quietly hope that when I did publish my e-mail address in the final column, I might be lucky enough to get some further feedback which might affirm the decision to create Adam, subject as I am to lingering doubts that he might just be a self-interested indulgence.

And so it is that, as of writing, I have had thousands of e-mail messages from all over the world, all bar two of them supportive. Before getting to the substance of how fabulous this has been I should get out of the way the fact that about 60 women and one bloke had taken "Widower of the Parish" as the world's longest and most detailed dating profile. Clearly some women had taken my revelation of sleeping with Lucy as permission to come clean about their own aspirations to get closer to Adam.

They would suggest that they "knew and trusted Adam", this being significant as probably eight out of 10 of the real online dating profiles I've ever seen list under "What I am looking for in a partner" the answer "Honesty" or "Integrity" or both! That they now should aspire to meet a faceless, emotionally fucked-up widower possibly suggests that other men on these sites are really unappealing or that these women are keen to go from frying pan to fire. Some of the mails had high-resolution photo attachments:

> *Adam, I don't normally do this sort of thing, I am a lawyer and really quite shy but since I know you are missing Helen so much here's a few pictures of me in my favourite Curvy Kate undies.*

The pictures, to be fair, were generally tasteful and accompanied by an invitation to meet up. OK, I quite enjoyed both the pictures and the offers – flattering probably not being the right word as they don't know if I look like Lurch from the Adams family!

I also hadn't realised I'd given such an impression that I live in Yorkshire; I don't, but a statistically significant number of my respondents were from that fair county. For the record I have not followed up a single one of these in-your-face propositions – life is complicated enough even if I had the energy or inclination.

By far the majority of messages and sincere sentiments have at times made my own journey look easy. Death in so many guises has filled often pages of harrowing, heartfelt description.

There are probably about 3000 people who have written to Adam, which by the 1:9:90 theory of digital engagement (1 person produces content: 9 comment on that content: 90 view that content), suggests that many more have taken some positives but not written to me. Unexpected! Of those 3000 or so e-mails I have received – they are still coming in – I'd segment them:

- 40% bereaved spouse/partner – for whom Adam's "move on but not leave behind" is a well-understood and much-liked sentiment.
- 15% bereaved other family member – including sons and daughters who are pleased to understand a little of what their parents went through.
- 15% spouse/partner of someone with a life-limiting illness – many looking for hope that there is a life beyond the worst happening to their loved one.
- 10% people who have an illness that they are unlikely to recover from – often seeing in Adam's story reassurance that their surviving loved one and family will be OK.
- 10% people who have a major, non-medical challenge – they are looking for hope and often simply want to "touch" someone who seems to be coping and so find new strength.
- 8% people who found the column was simply a good

read. Thank you all.
- 2% friendly women – often with cameras.

Percentages sound so clinical and underplay the raft of raw emotion floating through these letters. I have read them all and really want to reply to every single one. I feel a great guilt as with so little time I have only scraped the surface of doing so. But I will keep going, as so many are truly unforgettable, including a lady in Australia in the final stages of dying from fucking cancer who has been admitted to hospital and is not expected to leave. She tells me that her reading of the column somehow galvanised her to hold on and, as of writing, she is indeed back home. How, why and what that says I can only guess but it makes me feel glad, humbled and moved in a way that the old pre-diagnosis version of me wouldn't recognise. I have changed.

Even that story did not prepare me for the extraordinary and shocking mail from Hazel in Scotland:

Hazel: *Thank you for writing your column. I've been reading it since the very beginning with sympathy but never really thinking it would ever apply to me.*

She then tells me of the horrific freak accident which had killed her partner only a week earlier:

Hazel: *Right now I guess I'm still in shock. Over the last week there have been good days and terrible days and I* *suppose it'll be like that for a while...*

Reading your column today has reminded me that life will go on. I'm terrified by the road ahead but, on the other hand, the worst thing I could possibly imagine has already happened, so what's there to be scared of? Thank you again for sharing your story.

I was poleaxed at the proximity between his dying and her writing to me. I was also shamefully a little suspicious of it being a hoax but looking at her e-mail name and googling the accident details, sure enough the tragedy was reported exactly as she described. Poor woman. I wrote back offering any small support and comfort to someone so clearly in shock.

I am really grateful to her for writing. It made me truly understand that the whole business of death, unexpected or not, really is something no one thinks about or has any obvious point of support for when it happens. I now understand with full force that I truly am not alone and that much of my behaviour, which I thought weird/offensive/self-indulgent/too soon, turns out is not only acceptable but desirable as a means of dealing with grief in a way that others on their own grief journeys can relate to. My regret in all this is that the most constructive, caring, meaningful action that I will ever do in my life was writing the column, now this book, and that it is all over.

I want to believe that Helen would applaud the fact that her death and my way of dealing with it has brought some hope and comfort for others. I'm very grateful to

Harriet Green, formerly at *The Guardian*, for her faith in me and to so many family and friends for their help and comfort in being featured in the column, as well as keeping Adam's identity close to their chest.

This book, I hope, gets close to the column as a source of comfort, positivity and inspiration to bereaved comrades and non-bereaved civilians – normal people like we once were looking for relief that their lives are not so shit after all and maybe with a bit of extra insight from this book might even be a tad better!

Bereavement and the life-change it brings certainly need opening up and airing. More specifically I'm glad my story has been told so that in the future Millie and Matt can read it and say:

Millie/Matt: *Our dad was always cocking up but he did OK and didn't half love our mum.*

I am far from OK in many ways. Griefbergs and ambushes are still out there waiting malevolently in the shadows but I'm better at dealing with them.

Grief's darkness is part of the fabric of our lives but pales against the brightness of the hope and joy around it. Part of me believes that I am living now for two and that, somehow, Helen is here guiding me still as I steam on, head down against the storm, bringing Millie and Matt safely to port just as I promised her I would as she lay dying.

As a final thought I quote once again from the *Potter* books Helen so loved:

Sirius to Harry: *The ones that love us never really leave us. You can always find them.*

Thank you.

EPILOGUE

I have finished the book and feel a sense of both relief and sadness. The weeks of work and pressure to deliver something that would tell our story well had sat heavily at times. With the approaching new school year, Millie and Matt need me not to have my head in a laptop and I want to be able to live out my day-to-day life not wondering whether a new joy, irritant or person should "go in the book".

The morning is sunny and warm but these are not the scorching dog days of August; there's instead a sense of late-summer languor as the Siberians stretch out in the garden, not bothering to lift more than a long tail in response to the taunting birds.

I'm sending the finished manuscript to Pete, a tiny e-mail for such a lot of angst, having asked him to read it rapidly for a quick sense-check before it goes to the publisher. I know, as you now all know, he will be honest but kind, erring Yoda-wards in wordplay and just terrifyingly right. His is the opinion I've sought for all those reasons but also because he's second only to Helen and the kids in his mentions and I owe him first sight for all his help, and dare I say, love. He certainly lectures

Adam more than anyone and I thank him now as my writing ends and I press send.

Later. It's early evening and I'm standing at Helen's graveside placing flowers on her beautiful slate memorial. The air is chilly now, a reminder of the passing of the season and the ever-widening time since she and I last laughed together. My phone vibrates insistently, cutting into my quiet moment but hopefully not disturbing anyone else's in the near-deserted cemetery.

It's Pete. I decide on this one occasion to answer by Helen's graveside, somehow sensing it is the right thing to do.

Me: *What do you think?*
Pete: *I don't look like Yoda…*
Me: *Not now. I'm at Helen's memorial. Did you finish? What do you think?*
Pete: *Let me go on, please. I don't look like Yoda but I will accept some comparison instead with the owner of this thought, "Now this is not the end. It is not even the beginning of the end. But it is, perhaps, the end of the beginning". Bye.*

Pete ends the call on that, quite literally, Churchillian note. Turning my phone off, I look down at Helen for a long time, gathering my thoughts until they overflow just enough to give me voice. I whisper to no one and to all: "I love and fear he's right."

The End. The Beginning.

Appendix A:

10-STEP GUIDE TO SURVIVING BEREAVEMENT

1. **Love:** You cannot love someone who is dead exactly as you did when they were alive. It can take time to understand or accept this but if you don't, you end up like Miss Havisham unable to rebuild your life. Your love kept evolving from the day you met your partner, and their loss of physical form makes it different but not destroyed because as we all know true love prevails, even over grief.

2. **Children:** If you are lucky enough to have them, they will pull you along in the early days. Involve kids in your grief and don't put on a brave face for their sake. Children need permission to cry as much as encouragement to laugh. Thanks, Millie and Matt.

3. **Time:** Not really a great healer, whatever people say. The first year is literally shocking, but the second is harder. Grief and loss will never diminish in size, so suck up that thought as early as you can. Use the

passing of time to shape and enlarge the new world around your grief, so diminishing its dominance.

4. **Tears:** Don't beat yourself up about not crying. It will happen in time. I still can only really do so when triggered by another's loss rather than my own.

5. **Friends:** Some will step up and some will scarper. Don't judge any who vanish or panic too harshly – everyone processes grief differently. If you need new friends who "get it", join WAY (Widowed & Young).

6. **Counselling:** People who don't want it need it most, months or years later. It allows you to get over the guilt of surviving and the greater guilt that the future may be equally as happy as the past, albeit different. Recommended.

7. **Sex:** You are single, but don't hurt people or beat yourself up for finding it when you are ready. It doesn't matter whether you seek comfort and affirmation of your new life between the sheets or over the kitchen table. Preferably, you will manage both. It is bloody great. Physical closeness to another human body can heal deep wounds yet no one talks about it.

8. **Help:** Use the magic words "I need help" and people respond. It extends beyond family to friends and acquaintances if they have the skills and resources to give you domestic, financial, professional or whatever

aid. Works best in the first year when your loss is a big deal to all. True friends are there to be asked anytime.

9. **New love?:** Don't be surprised if the first single attractive member of the opposite sex who shows you kindness becomes an object of rather too much esteem. They are inadvertently planting attraction in your freshly tilled emotional seedbed. Hello, sister-in-loss Jo.

10. **Cancer:** It is always fucking cancer. It just is. Raise or give money if you can to fight the fucker. OK, this is a bit specific. Whatever your loved one died of, make it a villain and call it out often for what it is – it can be remarkably cathartic, no disrespect intended in any way. E.g. Crappy Coronary, Arsehole Accident, Bastard Bereavement sort of thing.

Appendix B:

10 Ways Anyone Can Be Happier

1. Measure Who Matters

I realise time is precious – I no longer believe I have the capacity to carry forward relationships with all the people I know and who have a call on my time, without under-investing in those who matter.

Action: Take an honest view of whom you want your limited time and attention to be directed towards and focus only there. It is painful but I now know it is ultimately liberating as you get more back from and give more to the people you love than from those you just like or know.

2. Love Your Life. Love Your Body

As sole parent I now need to live a long time for the kids but have been exposed to so much illness – of people struck in midlife not just by any one of the 100-plus fucking cancers but all manner of other dreadful stuff. Our bodies are remarkable and without health and viability we have nothing. This truth hides for most of us in full view and we carry the rampant invulnerability of youth into middle age until the shit hits the fan.

Action: Drink less, exercise more and go to the doctor to check you are well, not just when you are ill. If there is a family history of health issues investigate regularly even if you have to pay for it and bin a holiday. Yes, it's that deadly serious.

3. Never Say No to Fun

Knowing the kids may leave home in a few years and I'll be alone has made me more determined than ever to be there for them. We are a tight unit as three and when they want to play in the garden, go to the fair, shoot a Nerf gun or watch a film what they are asking is almost certainly more important than anything I'm doing, like the grouting or recycling.

Action: Make the default for the people you love "yes" not "later" when they want to spend time with you. It's now.

4. What's Your Future History?

I now ask myself this a lot. The concept of killing time for me is doing anything that doesn't positively impact on those I love. The truth of course is that time is killing us all daily and not to value every moment of it is wasting the gift of life. I have always believed that we should look ahead and set personal goals that we consciously and subconsciously head towards in our day-to-day lives.

Action: Draw a large picture on an A3 piece of paper of your own tombstone and write on it two things that you would want friends and relatives to say you have achieved in this life, then ask yourself how you are going to make sure they happen. A toughie but a goodie.

5. Sense & Sexuality
Curiously enough, this hardly gets mentioned as a way of rebooting your sense of what matters. Lie in your lover's arms and speak of your hopes and dreams and come the morning it might just start to happen or at least be less of a problem to talk about in daylight. While dating and needing to be discreet for Millie and Matt's sake, I have ended up having a quickie in, among other places, the garden shed, my glass studio (a bigger shed) and the back of the car (bit of a shed). This was thrilling, hilarious, very life-affirming and not at all sensible.

Action: Life-mentoring exercises don't always have to be cerebral. If your circumstances allow, then do it. Does it help long term? Who cares? Take the risk, it might just remind you that you are lucky enough to be alive and in love.

6. Stop!
The thing about bereavement is that you do a lot of thinking, drinking and staring into space, often alone, often at night. Not ideal behaviour but it helped me start to look at the world around me in all its beauty. This recalibration of consciousness and pace really helps me counter the massive busyness I've created as a grief-coping mechanism and still does beyond those dark early days. The clue that it would lives in *Ferris Bueller's Day Off*:

Ferris: *Life moves pretty fast. If you don't stop and look around once in a while, you could miss it.*

Action: *Turn the phone off and spend just five minutes every day at different times simply watching the world – the sun, sky, nature, streets, people.*

7. Think Small

Author Bill Bryson seeded this for me in his *Notes from a Small Island* when he described how we Brits take our pleasures small – "Before long I came to regard all kinds of activities – asking for more toast in a hotel, buying wool-rich socks at Marks & Spencer, getting two pairs of trousers when I only really needed one – as something daring, very nearly illicit. My life became immensely richer."

If you can take your pleasures small some of the time you will never be unhappy and doing so makes downsizing jobs and income less of a challenge. A key component of doing so is noticing the small stuff in the beautiful world in which we live.

Action: *Open your eyes and think about the sensual pleasures that really make you happy and how many of them are free, small, already around you.*

8. Think Big

Do not as I did but as I say. I always knew that this one was going to be a stretch, as I didn't crack it until I was forced to by Helen's death. I had set up businesses in my past but where they failed it was because I was not prepared to risk giving up the day job and focusing on them. My "circles of comfort" were too well established to break out of until events and fucking cancer intervened.

Action: Identify what big ambition you have in your life – work, home, family. Ask yourself "Why not you? Why not now?" and see how you might stand out of your circle of comfort and push aside the natural negativity we all can suffer from as we seek to protect the status quo. Then find and take a first step, however small, to fulfilling your dream.

9. Work Yourself happy

I was lucky in that I loved what I did for a long time but my close encounter with Helen's illness made me reconsider my priorities which were then largely about my children. Since then I have ended up planning my own business as no employment has so far won me over – with the brutal new perspective of the bereaved, I now see work as renting out my most precious commodity, the remaining time of my life, which sets the bar pretty high. We all may work up to 99,000 hours in a lifetime – more than 11 years – that's a lot of yourself to be selling.

Action: Are you getting enough out of your job to justify the price you are paying your employer to have it – your very life? If not, look to 8.

10. Write on

I have benefited so much from writing the "Widower" column both in dealing with my grief journey and rebuilding myself along the way. Not a writer historically, I now write daily, just a few lines, but it has changed the way I think about living my life. Try it and you'll never stop.

Action: I'm calling this the two-week challenge as even if you hate it at first stick it out for two weeks and then see how you feel. I hope you'll keep at it.

Every night take out your phone and e-mail yourself the answer to the following three questions using no more than six words for each:

a.   Today – what made me truly happy?
b.   Today – what did I do well?
c.   Today – what would I change about it?

The more adventurous of you might choose to use a dedicated Twitter account to record your thoughts. A parchment and quill is also cool.

Review all your answers for the past seven days each week when you are putting out the bins – find your own ritual – and think about the trajectory of your life and happiness. The DNA of any fixes probably lies somewhere in the other nine exercises you are already doing.

Good luck!

Adam Golightly (pseudonym) is a Northerner who lives in Hertfordshire with his two teenage children and three cats. A recent widower, he wrote a weekly column last year in *The Guardian* about adjusting to his new life as a lone parent and single man. @mradamgolightly